Transcending Ego:
Distinguishing Consciousness from Wisdom

TRANSCENDING EGO: DISTINGUISHING CONSCIOUSNESS FROM WISDOM
(Tib. *namshe yeshe gepa*)

A Treatise of the Third Karmapa
RANGJUNG DORJE

With a Commentary by
THE VENERABLE KHENCHEN THRANGU RINPOCHE
Geshe Lharampa

Translated by Peter Alan Roberts

Namo Buddha Publications

Namo Buddha Publications
P. O. Box 778
Glastonbury, CT 06033
E-mail: info@NamoBuddhaPub.com
Website: www.NamoBuddhaPub.com

Second Edition
ISBN 978-1-931571-21-0

Printed in the United States on acid-free, FSC certified paper.

The Table of Contents

Acknowledgments

First we wish to express our sincere thanks to Khenchen Thrangu Rinpoche for giving these teachings. We would also like to thank Peter Alan Roberts for translating the root text and Thrangu Rinpoche's commentary, Gaby Hollmann for transcribing and editing the teachings, and Sarah Harding and Linda Hebenstreit for painstakingly checking the manuscript. We would also like to thank Pönlop Rinpoche for his advice on the manuscript.

Note

To help the Buddhist practitioner, the Tibetan words are given as they are pronounced, not spelled. Their actual spelling can be found in the Glossary of Tibetan Terms.

We use the convention of BCE (Before Current Era) for "B. C." and CE (Current Era) for "A. D."

Rangjung Dorje, the Third Karmapa (1284-1339 CE)
Author of *The Treatise Distinguishing Consciousness from Wisdom*

Editor's Foreword

Two and a half millennia ago the Buddha proposed that all our happiness and all our suffering are due to one thing: our mind. After reaching realization he spent the rest of his life giving teachings on how we can work with the mind to achieve complete peace, nirvana, or enlightenment.

The basic method for working with mind is through meditation. The Buddha began by teaching tranquility (Skt. *shamatha*) and insight (Skt. *vipashyana*) meditation, which are practiced by Buddhists all over the world. This path, called the sutra path, is a very steady and gradual path. Except in the case of a few exceptional individuals, it takes many lifetimes of meditation to achieve enlightenment using the practices of the sutra path. To practice the Buddhist teachings, regardless of sect or style, one should begin by practicing the accumulation of great merit, the development of pure conduct, and engaging in shamatha and vipashyana meditation. There are many excellent books on the sutra path by great Theravada teachers, Zen masters, and Tibetan lamas. Thrangu Rinpoche's *The Practice of Tranquillity and Insight* is one of these books.

Another path leading to enlightenment is the Vajrayana path. If one applies oneself with great effort to the practice of the Vajrayana, it is possible to achieve enlightenment rapidly. As pointed out many times by Thrangu Rinpoche, the goal of awakening or enlightenment is exactly the same for all paths. The choice is in the method one pursues. Both the sutra and Vajrayana methods have been extensively practiced in Tibet. One of the most important Vajrayana meditations is the meditation of the Mahamudra or "great seal," which involves looking directly at the mind. To understand mahamudra meditation, it is important to identify our mental processes. The examination of the nature of mind, how thoughts arise, where they dwell and disappear leads to profound insights on the path.

This text on consciousness and wisdom is a detailed map of what is perceived when one engages in this process of looking into the mind. Rangjung Dorje, one of the great Buddhist thinkers of his time, brings together in this text the Abhidharma literature of the Theravadins, the emptiness teachings of the Middle-way, the Mind-only writings of the Chittamatrins, and the practice of examining mind directly through Mahamudra. He begins with a description of the eight mental consciousnesses and describes each in terms of what it does and how it leads us to perceive our world incorrectly. Because these eight consciousnesses cause us to see the world in a deluded way, we continue to live in samsara and this causes us to continue to experience unhappiness, frustration, dissatisfaction, and emotional upheavals. After this description of the eight consciousnesses he explains how these are transformed into the five wisdoms that manifest in the mind at the time of the attainment of enlightenment.

Central to all discussions on the nature of reality in the Mahayana and Vajrayana levels of Buddhism is the concept of emptiness. Emptiness (Skt. *shunyata*) is actually the fundamental characteristic of material phenomena. This is treated slightly differently in two traditions in Tibet. One tradition, the Shentong tradition, to greatly simplify, holds that Buddha-nature pervades all sentient beings and it is this *tathagatagarbha* which is the potential for all sentient beings to reach buddhahood. The Rangtong tradition holds that everything is empty of inherent existence and so Buddha-nature cannot exist in everyone as a permanent quality. These slightly different views of the Shentong and Rangtong traditions are given in more detail in Hookham's book *The Buddha Within*. This treatise by Rangjung Dorje is an important text of the Shentong view, which differs slightly from the Rangtong presentation of consciousness and wisdom. In addition, Rangjung Dorje held a few views that were different from the traditional Mind-only or Chittamatra view. The presentation, particularly of the transformation of the actual consciousnesses into wisdoms, is based on Rangjung Dorje's realization. To make sure the Shentong view was properly represented, Thrangu Rinpoche reviewed the section on the transformation of consciousnesses into wisdoms to make sure the text conforms exactly to what Rangjung Dorje had proposed.

The Treatise Distinguishing Consciousness from Wisdom, like most other texts on Mahamudra practice, is not in the form of a scholarly thesis, but is in the form of a song of realization, or *doha*. A spiritual song distills the realization of the Vajrayana practitioner into verse, with each line usually having nine syllables. This particular text is very compact and comprises only thirty-six verses. In the nineteenth century the great scholar Jamgon Kongtrul wrote a longer commentary on this treatise to help clarify its meaning. Thrangu Rinpoche consulted Jamgon Kongtrul's commentary when he taught on this spiritual song.

In the Tibetan tradition a student first memorizes these root verses as a part of his or her religious studies. The student then requests a lama, known not only for his or her scholarly accomplishment and understanding of the text but also for his realizations, to give a lengthy line-by-line commentary on the root text. Presented in this text is a translation of this great vajra song and a commentary by Thrangu Rinpoche, an eminent scholar of Buddhism who possesses the above qualities. With this text, the Western student of Buddhism can have the experience of being able to study a profound text with a commentary by an excellent scholar of Tibetan Buddhism, just as students in the Buddhist monasteries of Tibet have done for the past millennium.

Distinguishing Consciousness from Wisdom is an important text on psychology as well as Buddhist philosophy. Rangjung Dorje arrives at conclusions about how the mind works which are far different from what modern Western psychology would suggest. To illustrate this, I will briefly summarize the arguments of the text, not in the order presented in the text, but in a Western framework.

First, Buddhist meditators have reported since the first century of our era that everything is insubstantial or empty of inherent nature. Physicists in the twentieth century have put forward a similar conclusion. We are told in modern physics that matter is not made up of solid particles but is actually made up of energy patterns. The physicist Bohm has said poetically, "matter is crystallized light." It is well known that solid objects are actually 99.99% "empty" space and the atoms that make up solid objects are actually moving at incredible speeds. Rangjung Dorje in this text begins his exposition by refuting the view that a god or gods created a solid universe and asserts that instead, the universe that we conceive of as solid, real objects outside us, which definitely appear and interact with us on the relative level, ultimately are insubstantial or "empty," like a rainbow or a reflection in a mirror.

The second argument is that Buddhist meditators have known from at least the fourth century of our era that it is the human mind, or more specifically, human awareness, that has created the illusion of a solid universe. They point out that individuals have reincarnated for thousands of lifetimes, that in each of these lives they have had extensive experience with material objects, and that these experiences have been stored in their minds (in what is called the "eighth consciousness"). In Western psychology the scientific proof of reincarnation lies in the methodology of past life regression, and it is unfortunate that hard scientific investigation has yet to be done to demonstrate whether individuals in this lifetime can recall events and facts about their previous lives that were not gained by any source in this lifetime. Who better to make the argument for reincarnation than the author of this song of realization, the Karmapa? The Karmapa, for the past sixteen lifetimes, has written a letter a few years before his death; and in this letter, which is not opened until several years after his death, he predicts his name, the name of his parents, and where they can find him. So far the letter has always been accurate, demonstrating that he knows reincarnation at a level far beyond our understanding.

Since human beings have had similar experiences, they therefore "see" and experience the world in a similar fashion. To use Michael Talbot's analogy, our mind has created the solidity of the hologram so that when we run into a brick wall, which is really an energy projection like a hologram, we bounce off it and are hurt. While we may argue with the holographic theory, Amit Goswami, the author of a widely used textbook in quantum mechanics, has taken data from physics and summarized it in *The Self-Aware Universe: How Consciousness Creates the Material Universe*. So we see that when Rangjung Dorje describes how mind creates the universe based on his study of the Mind-only school, he is not far from theories explored by modern physics some 700 years later.

Third, the *alaya* consciousness, first described in the fourth century by the Mind-only school of Buddhism, stores all our impressions and karmic latencies, and this makes it possible for us to function. If we look at a piece of metal that is of gold and shows a man seated cross-legged touching the ground, we immediately think, "a statue of the Buddha." But how did we know it was the Buddha or even who the Buddha was? We must have stored somewhere in our mind some previous experience where someone told us who the Buddha was. This then is one function of the alaya consciousness. Wilder Penfield, a Canadian neurosurgeon working with epileptics, has presented evidence that we store every sensory impression we experience in the brain. Rangjung Dorje, citing the Mind-only school, goes much further than this and says that the alaya consciousness stores impressions over many lifetimes, which obviously places the alaya consciousness outside of the brain.

Fourth, the alaya consciousness has been treated by all meditators as being empty of nature. We feel that we possess a solid and real mind, but this mind is merely a continuity of an ever-changing stream. This means the mind for Buddhists is not a permanent self or *atman* in the Hindu sense or a soul in the Christian sense. This consciousness not only stores the impressions from many lifetimes, but it also stores the karmic latencies of these experiences. This fact is very important for meditators, because if the eighth consciousness didn't store these latencies, there would be no cause and effect of our actions, and essentially we could do anything we wanted to do with no fear of consequences (except for what the authorities found out). However, there is karma, so Buddhists on the path must engage with great diligence to have only positive impressions and latencies enter their alaya consciousness. When we meet the Dalai Lama or some other realized person, we can feel the goodness and compassion radiating from them. This is not because they have been doing some special practice, but rather that they have been diligently working with their mind to accumulate positive karma.

Fifth, these latencies or impressions leave the alaya consciousness in two ways. First, when we dream, these karmic latencies appear to the mental consciousness, and the mental consciousness takes them to be real phenomena. Second, when sense impressions from our sense faculties reach the mental consciousness, the mental consciousness combines these with the latencies from the alaya consciousness and they appear real and solid to us, although outer phenomena are actually not solid and real. It is this process of mind that leads great Buddhist meditators to tell us that our experience of external phenomena is created by mind and that our world is actually an illusion.

Sixth, with great diligence of having only positive impressions and latencies enter the alaya consciousness and with strong meditation, we can actually purify the alaya consciousness to the point that our ordinary consciousnesses transform into the five wisdoms of enlightenment. Then we are no longer bound by our material circumstance and have actually transcended samsaric entrapment. At this point a great master such as Milarepa can put his hand through solid objects because he has completely realized that they are in fact empty. It is only our latent impressions over hundreds of lifetimes that have made external phenomena solid and "real" for us.

Clearly, this summary is a very cursory account of Buddhist psychology. Eastern and Western psychology is difficult to reconcile because these two psychologies rely on entirely different assumptions. It also shows how modern and relevant Rangjung Dorje's text is even though it was written seven hundred years ago.

Thrangu Rinpoche's commentary on this text was given at two different occasions: at the Namo Buddha Summer Seminar in Oxford, England in September, 1989 and at the Namo Buddha Winter Seminar in January of 1990 in Nepal. The presentation here includes the combined teachings to make it a thorough commentary on this important work.

Clark Johnson, PhD

Translator's Preface

Prior to the time of the Buddha (c. 490-410 BCE) the *Brahmanas* and the earliest *Upanishads* of the Vedic tradition in India presented enumerations of the constituents that comprised an individual's mind and faculties, such as the eight pranas described in the *Brihadaranyaka Upanishad*: the prana of breath, eye, speech, tongue, ear, body, mind (*manas*), all of which arose from and were reabsorbed into an underlying *atman* (soul or self).

The Buddha, who referred to and refuted the *Brihadaranyaka Upanishad*, denied the existence of the underlying atman, but enumerated the constituents of the empirical individual in his doctrine of five aggregates (*skandhas*), or six consciousnesses.

All the early Buddhist traditions that developed from the third century BCE onwards preserved the teaching of six consciousnesses. In particular, a systematizing doctrine based on the Buddha's sutras attempted to present a numeric delineation of the constituents of existence. This was known as the Abhidharma tradition, and the Vaibhashika school considered certain Abhidharma texts to be the words of the Buddha. The Tripitaka or "Three Baskets" were formed through conjoining the Abhidharma to the collection of the sutras together with the Buddha's teachings on monastic rules, the Vinaya. Other philosophical schools, such as the Sautrantika, however, refused to recognize the canonical authenticity of the Abhidharma, which was given commentarial status only.

All Tibetan Buddhist traditions recognize the supremacy of the Sautrantika amongst the early schools of Buddhism; therefore, there is no Abhidharma section in the Kangyur, the Tibetan canon of the Buddha's words. All Abhidharma texts are found only in the Tengyur, the Tibetan translations of Indian Buddhist treatises and commentaries. The principal treatise in this canon is the *Treasury of the Abhidharma* (*Abhidharma-kosha*) by Vasubandhu (fourth to fifth centuries CE).

The Madhyamaka (Middle-way) tradition, which was promulgated especially by Nagarjuna (second or third century CE), also taught the six consciousnesses. Later Madhyamaka masters such as Chandrakirti (seventh century) and Shantideva (circa 675-715 CE), who are referred to by Thrangu Rinpoche in this book, maintained this view, denying the validity of the two additional consciousnesses introduced by the Chittamatra (Mind-only) school promulgated especially by Asanga (fourth century) and by his younger brother Vasubandhu in his later Mahayana works, such as *The Thirty Verses,* a key source for Rangjung Dorje's *The Treatise Distinguishing Consciousness and Wisdom.*

The eighth century witnessed the rise of a syncretism of Madhyamaka and Chittamatra, such as that taught by Shantarakshita. Shantarakshita came to Tibet in 762 CE and was instrumental in establishing Buddhism there. As a result of this unification of differing views, scholars began to divide the Buddha's teachings into those in which the meaning is explicit and those in which the meaning is implicit. In the latter category, the apparent meaning was therefore considered to be expedient. This new method of classification allowed scholars to consider the body of the Buddha's teachings as a unified hierarchy of what otherwise would appear to be contradictory views.

In addition, by the eleventh century, the higher tantra tradition had introduced a system of five buddha families. The numerical equivalence with the five aggregates facilitated a teaching of the transmutation of specific aggregates to corresponding wisdoms. This teaching is found, for example, in the fourteenth century *terma,* the *Bardo Todrol,* better known as *The Tibetan Book of the Dead.* In this system all eight consciousnesses are included within the aggregate of consciousness, and so all eight transform into *dharmadhatu* wisdom. In turn, each of the other aggregates transforms as follows: form transforms into mirror-wisdom, the aggregate of sensation into equality wisdom, the aggregate of identification into discriminating wisdom, and the aggregate of mental activity into accomplishment wisdom. Rangjung Dorje's text, however, presents a less well-known alternative. According to this text, the aggregate of consciousness alone transforms into all five wisdoms.

Rangjung Dorje (1284-1339) was the third in the lineage of Karmapa reincarnations, the supreme hierarchs of the Karma Kagyu school, which commenced with Düsum Khyenpa (1110-1193). He composed *The Treatise Distinguishing Consciousness and Wisdom* in 1323 CE based particularly on the writings of Asanga and Vasubandhu.

The commentator to this text, Jamgon Kongtrul (1813-1899), was a prolific commentator, compiler, and editor of Buddhist teachings, especially of the Karma Kagyu tradition. He wrote commentaries for all three of Rangjung Dorje's texts: *The Profound Inner Meaning, The Treatise Elucidating Buddha-Nature*, and this work, *The Treatise Distinguishing Consciousness and Wisdom*. Jamgon Kongtrul's commentary on the latter text is entitled *An Adornment for Rangjung Dorje's Thoughts*. It is this commentary which served as the basis for Thrangu Rinpoche's teaching on the Third Karmapa's text.

In 1959, in order to escape from the holocaust of Chinese Communist oppression unleashed at that time, the eighth Thrangu Rinpoche (born in 1933) had to leave Thrangu Monastery in east Tibet. He fled to India where he became the Khenpo and principal teacher of scholastic studies at Rumtek monastery in Sikkim, where Rangjung Dorje, the Sixteenth Karmapa (1924-1981), had established his seat in exile. Subsequently, Thrangu Rinpoche founded Thrangu Tashi Choeling monastery, Thrangu Tara Abbey nunnery, and Shree Mangal Dvip School in Kathmandu; Thrangu Tashi Yangtse monastery in Namo Buddha in Nepal; and the Vajra Vidya Institute in Sarnath, India. Since 1979 he has toured the world extensively, establishing Buddhist centers in the far east, Europe and North America, in particular Thrangu Monastery in Vancouver.

Peter Alan Roberts

Table 1

The Five Aggregates of Consciousness
(Skt. skandha; Tib. pung po)

The Aggregate	The Sanskrit	The Tibetan*
FORM		
1. form	rupa	gzugs
NAME		
2. feeling	vadana	tshor ba
3. identification	samjna	'du shes
4. mental formation	samskara	'du byed
5. consciousness	vijnana	rnam shes

The Tibetan words are given as they are spelled, not pronounced.

In Buddhism all outside phenomena that we perceive and all internal perception of this phenomena in our minds are called "name and form." They have been categorized as the five aggregates (literally "heaps" or "piles"). The first aggregate is all outside phenomena such as sights, sounds, and body sensations. These enter the sense organ and the appropriate sense consciousness and in the second aggregate the feeling of "like, dislike, neutral" develops. Then in the third aggregate the object is identified. The object is connected to all our experience with the object in the fourth aggregate. Finally, in the fifth aggregate it enters our mental consciousness where it becomes part of our thoughts.

Chapter 1

An Introduction to the Text

There are four major traditions of Tibetan Buddhism: the Kagyu, Sakya, Nyingma, and Gelug. Each school has its own particular approach. The Gelug school, for example, emphasizes learning and scholarship, whereas the Kagyu school emphasizes practice and is known, therefore, as the *drubgyu* or "practice lineage" school. The principle meditation of the Kagyu lineage is the *Mahamudra*[1] or "great seal." The Mahamudra instructions came from Saraha (ninth to tenth century CE), Tilopa (928-1009 CE), and Naropa (956-1040 CE). They taught through the method of pith spiritual songs or *dohas*. These spiritual songs do not give a detailed presentation of Buddhism but use poetical imagery to introduce the listener to the nature of the mind. Spiritual songs express these practice instructions in the form of poetry. They are very brief and direct and are very beneficial to the mind. Although they contain actual Buddhist philosophical teachings, the emphasis is on the recognition of the nature of the mind.

Gampopa (1079-1153 CE), the Tibetan master who founded the monastic order of the Kagyu school, unified the teachings of the Mahamudra tradition with the scholastic and monastic Kadam tradition of Atisha (982-1055 CE). Gampopa taught that the study of Maitreya's *Uttaratantra* would be a great help for comprehending the Mahamudra instructions on the direct experience of the nature of one's mind.

Gampopa's principal pupil, Düsum Khyenpa (1110-1193 CE), was the First Karmapa and founder of the Karma Kagyu school, which has since been governed by successive Karmapa rebirths. The Third Karmapa, Rangjung Dorje (1284-1339), composed a text entitled *The Profound Inner Meaning*. In it he described the subtle

1

channels and subtle winds that exist within the body and how these winds and channels are the basis for the practice of meditation.² He also composed two other very short texts: *The Treatise Distinguishing Consciousness and Wisdom*, which is the text we are concerned with here, and a summary of the *Uttaratantra* entitled *A Treatise Elucidating Buddha-nature*. Rangjung Dorje said that if we can understand the *Uttaratantra* with these two short texts, we will be able to comprehend mahamudra meditation.

THE EIGHT CONSCIOUSNESSES: AN OVERVIEW

The Treatise Distinguishing Consciousness from Wisdom assumes that we have familiarity with the doctrine of the eight consciousnesses. Therefore, before explaining the treatise itself, I shall give a brief description of the eight consciousnesses.

The first teachings given by the Buddha were those of the Foundation vehicle now practiced primarily by Theravada Buddhists. These teachings enumerated six different kinds of consciousness. First, there are five consciousnesses associated with the five physical sensory organs: the visual consciousness of the eye, the auditory consciousness of the ear, the olfactory consciousness of the nose, the gustatory consciousness of the tongue, and the tactile consciousness of the body. These five sensory consciousnesses directly perceive the external objects of visual forms, sounds, smells, tastes, and body sensations without any conceptual differentiation of these phenomena into good and bad, pleasant and unpleasant, and so on. They are nonconceptual consciousnesses of direct perception.

The sixth consciousness is the mental consciousness, which engages with the perceptions of the five sensory consciousnesses. In the Buddhist science of epistemology and logic called the *Pramana*, the mental consciousness is defined as a conceptual consciousness. It is the mental consciousness that defines a visual perception, for example, as being good or bad, large or small, and so forth. So first, an object is perceived by the eye and apprehended by the visual consciousness. This then passes on to the mental consciousness, which then conceptualizes, "This is good" or "This is big." This categorization goes on, of course, for the perceptions of the other four sensory consciousnesses.

The mental consciousness does not have the ability of direct perception. So, for example, if we see a bell, the visual consciousness produces a visual image of the bell but doesn't apprehend the name "bell" or its characteristics. The mental consciousness, however, apprehends a mental image of the bell, not as a visual image, but in reliance on the concept of "bell" and its specific characteristics. For example, the visual consciousness can see only one side of a door. The mental consciousness, however, can join many instances of perceiving the door and thus can conceive a mental image of the front, back, inside, and outside of the door.

The five external sensory consciousnesses are like a mute who can see. Although a mute person can see everything, he cannot describe what he has seen. The mental consciousness, on the other hand, is said to be like a blind person who can speak: he is able to describe things, but he cannot directly perceive them.

The Buddhist teaching on the six consciousnesses refuted the pre-Buddhist doctrines that assert the existence of a single consciousness. These non-Buddhist theories held that there is only one consciousness, although it may seem as if there are many. They gave the example of a monkey inside a house with six windows. Sometimes the monkey looks out the east window, sometimes out the north window, then out the west window, and so on. An observer on the outside might think that there are six monkeys in that house, even though in fact there is only one. This example was given to explain how one consciousness could process information from the five sensory and the mental consciousnesses.

The Buddha postulated a different view. He countered that there were six distinct consciousnesses, each with its own particular characteristics. The Buddha taught that if there were only one monkey inside the house, when it looked out of an eastern window, for example, then all the other windows would be empty. But when we see something with our eyes, our ears do not become deaf. When we listen with our ears, our eyes do not become blind. We can see, hear, and smell simultaneously, within the same instant, therefore six separate consciousnesses can be identified.

These consciousnesses were described by the Buddha to be aggregates (Skt. *skandhas*), not single units. For example, when we perceive different colors, such as yellow, red, or white, one consciousness does not perceive all these colors; instead, a different aggregate of visual consciousness perceives each color. Similarly, there are also different visual consciousnesses for shapes. In the same way, an aggregation of auditory consciousnesses is itself an aggregation of a multitude of momentary consciousness perceiving different sounds. Similarly, a collection of tactile aggregates experiences the sensations of hands, feet, and other body parts simultaneously.[3] The sixth, mental consciousness is also made of many parts, because the mind can conceive of many different things such as past, present, and future.

The six consciousnesses are impermanent. A visual consciousness does not last from morning to evening. The visual consciousness of an image arises for only an instant; it then ceases and is immediately followed by another visual consciousness that lasts for only an instant. Therefore these six consciousnesses are aggregates of successive momentary experiences.

As well as being impermanent, the five sensory and the mental consciousness are classed as temporary because they are not always present. For example, when one closes one's eyes there is no longer a visual consciousness perceiving visual images. The mental consciousness is also characterized by the quality of luminosity (Tib. *salwa*)[4] and clearly perceives the object, while the seventh and eighth consciousnesses are not as vivid and apparent. The seventh and eighth consciousnesses are classed as being "ever-present but unclear" while the first six consciousness are classed as "temporary, but vivid."

In the Mahayana teachings the Buddha described two additional consciousnesses. The seventh consciousness is called the "afflicted consciousness," and it functions basically as clinging to a self. This consciousness is very subtle in that it does not need to specifically think, "Is this me?" Instead, it is continuously and latently present, clinging to a self whether a visual, auditory, gustatory, olfactory, or kinesthetic perception is taking place. This contrasts with the mental consciousness where the feeling of self is very conscious and discernible. The afflicted seventh consciousness is a neutral obscuration and in itself is neither positive nor negative. It does not create good or bad karma. Nevertheless, the belief in a self directly opposes the wisdom of realizing egolessness.[5] This affliction is the principle obstacle that must be removed to attain liberation.

The eighth consciousness is called the "ground consciousness;" it too is an aspect of luminosity and understanding that is ever present. No matter what kind of sensory perception occurs, this underlying continuity of consciousness is there. The ground consciousness is the basis, the ground, for all the other consciousnesses. It can be analyzed in terms of mind and mental events. Five mental events arise from the ground consciousness: form, feeling, identification, formation, and consciousness.[6] In the case of the seventh consciousness there are nine mental events: the above five as well as clinging to self, attachment to self, pride in self, and ignorance in relation to self. These mental events are like the transformations or the movements of the consciousnesses. When we look thoroughly and directly at the mind, we can identify each of these consciousnesses.

Among the eight consciousnesses, the mental consciousness is the most important. The visual consciousness may see an image that may or may not be beautiful, the ear consciousness may hear a pleasant or unpleasant sound, and so on, but it is the mental consciousness that decides if the sensory perception is beautiful or ugly. The liking of a perception brings about joy and attachment and gives rise to the afflictions or disturbing emotions (Skt. *kleshas*).[7] Experiencing an unpleasant sensory perception brings suffering and a disturbance of mental clarity. When meditating, we use our mental consciousness to calm and pacify the mind. Meditation pacifies all sensations and experiences of happiness and suffering, of attachment and aversion. When all sensations have been pacified, the mind is clear and peaceful. We then rest in this clear and peaceful state. This completely natural and true state of the mind is ultimate wisdom. When this state of wisdom is attained, all the eight consciousnesses are transformed into the five wisdoms.

This text describes the consciousnesses, explains how they function, and defines the nature of the five wisdoms in detail; therefore, it is called *The Treatise Distinguishing Consciousness from Wisdom*.

THE TITLE

The Treatise

The body of Buddhist literature can be divided into two categories: the discourses given by the Buddha himself, which are called the "Buddha's words," or *ka* in Tibetan, and the subsequent commentaries written by the Buddhist masters, or *shastra* in Sanskrit. The word shastra was translated into Tibetan as *tenchö*. The Tibetan word *chö* means "to correct;" a shastra corrects ignorance, error, and delusion in the mind and changes them into wisdom. The shastra accomplishes this by teaching (Tib. *ten*) the true nature clearly. When the truth is understood, the mind is automatically corrected. Thus, a treatise is called *tenchö* in Tibetan, meaning "correction through teaching." This text is therefore a shastra, a tenchö that clearly teaches the nature of consciousness and wisdom in order to dispel our ignorance and delusion.

Distinguishing

Rangjung Dorje differentiates consciousness from wisdom in this treatise by classifying them according to their respective natures. He does this in order to provide us with the knowledge necessary for successful meditation.

Consciousness

It is due to consciousness that we do not have ultimate knowledge. The Tibetan word for consciousness is *namshe*. This term was derived from the Sanskrit *vijnana*. The Sanskrit word *vijnana* means "complete knowing," with the first syllable *vi* meaning "total" and the second syllable *jnana* meaning "knowledge."

Consciousness does not create ignorance. It is a state of luminosity or intelligence of mind. However, what should be seen (i.e. the true nature of phenomena) is not perceived by consciousness. Rather, false appearances are what consciousness vividly perceives. This results in a state of delusion that obscures the realization of ultimate wisdom.

6

from Wisdom

The Tibetan word for wisdom is *yeshe*, which is a translation of the Sanskrit word *jnana*. The Sanskrit term, however, can also mean ordinary knowledge, the equivalent to the Tibetan word *shepa*. Therefore, the Tibetans translated *jnana* as "ultimate wisdom" and added *ye*, which means "primordial," to *she*, thus forming *yeshe*, which means "primordial wisdom."

The reason that we meditate is to transform our confused mind: to change our ignorance into wisdom, our erroneous beliefs into true knowledge. We practice to change from being under the influence of the negative emotions to being free from these negativities. So we are trying to change our impure state into a pure state. The impure state is the mind; the pure state is also mind. They are both mind, but there is a great difference between these two states of mind. The impure states are termed consciousnesses (*namshe*), and the pure states are termed wisdoms (*yeshe*). If we can clearly understand the difference between consciousness and wisdom, then our subsequent meditation practice will be free from error and delusion. This treatise on *Distinguishing Consciousness from Wisdom* is, therefore, very important for the practice of meditation to yield truth on the path.

THE HOMAGE

1. I pay homage to all the buddhas and bodhisattvas![8]

The treatise commences with the homage and the commitment to compose the text. Traditionally, from the time that early Buddhist masters composed shastras in India until the present time, Buddhist treatises have begun this way. Rangjung Dorje therefore begins his treatise with homage to the worthy recipients, who are the buddhas and the bodhisattvas.

The Buddha's teachings are divided into three sections: the Vinaya (the instructions on correct conduct), the Sutras (the words of the Buddha), and the Abhidharma (a systematic classification of the teachings). A specific homage is associated with each of these three different types of teachings. This treatise belongs to the category of sutra teachings, which are principally concerned with meditation, and the traditional homage for a sutra text is "I pay homage to all the buddhas and bodhisattvas." Thus this homage is paid to the Buddha, who taught the perfect Dharma, and also to the bodhisattvas who are the practitioners of those teachings. This homage is made to ensure that there will be no impediments to the completion of the text and to ensure that it will benefit many people.

Rangjung Dorje pays homage to the Buddha, who taught how to pacify all mental afflictions and sensations. Rangjung Dorje also pays homage to the bodhisattvas, those beings who practice the Buddha's teachings. So by showing respect and devotion to the buddhas and bodhisattvas, one's confidence in the teachings grows. By having a firm confidence in the teachings, one will practice them, and by practicing the teachings, one will achieve the goal of buddhahood.

THE COMMITMENT TO COMPOSE THE TEXT

2. *I gained a thorough understanding through hearing the teachings*
   And contemplating them.
   I then resided in solitude, in order to engage
   In the process of meditation. I shall describe here,
   The kind of realization that arose at that time.

This verse expresses Rangjung Dorje's commitment to compose the text. On an explicit level, Rangjung Dorje describes the process that resulted in his writing this text. Implicitly, these lines instruct us to do as he has done. It is as if he is saying, "This is what my followers should do in the future." Rangjung Dorje was an emanation of Avalokiteshvara, yet he humbly describes himself as an ordinary being. He says that he did not know how to practice properly, so it was first necessary to develop an understanding of the words of the Buddha and the commentaries. Unable to do this by himself, he studied with a master to gain the understanding that arises from listening to the teachings.

We shouldn't believe in something just because the Buddha or some great scholar or lama says so. We need a very clear and profound conviction that the Buddha's teachings are correct, and this is gained by using analysis and our own intelligence. Therefore, after our teacher has taught us the path, we should analyze and thoroughly contemplate the teachings and so gain the second type of understanding, which arises from this contemplation. This understanding based on listening and contemplation is not enough—this alone cannot transform our mind. This final transformation is accomplished by the practice of meditation. How do we meditate properly? This is described with the words, "I then resided in solitude." Having developed complete certainty in the teachings, Rangjung Dorje then meditated on the teachings in order to change his mind. He meditated in a solitary place so that all the movements of his mind and the unstable thoughts would disappear and transform into wisdom. Through his meditation he was able to completely understand and answer these questions. He realized how important it would be for others to understand the nature of consciousness and the five wisdoms, so he composed this text. Rangjung Dorje teaches us by example that we too should learn to see the nature of consciousness and wisdom through hearing and contemplating the teachings. Then we should follow this with meditation in solitude.

We can't achieve realization on our own. If we meditate with our inadequate understanding, we won't be able to develop genuine meditation. Instead we need the help of someone who has had the experience of meditation; that someone is the Buddha. He taught about the nature of meditation, gave the methods of meditation, and taught the purpose of meditation. We must first listen[9] to the teachings of the Buddha, and then we must understand the teachings by contemplating them. After developing a definite understanding, we then have to meditate on the teachings. So we must do all three together—listen, contemplate, and meditate—in order to progress.

The Buddha taught that we must meditate to achieve realization. For example, we cannot convince someone that molasses is sweet by repeatedly telling them that it is sweet. Even though the person may understand our words, until that person personally tastes it, he or she will not have the experience of the sweet taste. It is the same for Dharma; we can listen to the teachings for a long time and contemplate them, but without meditation we cannot actually experience them. If, however, we taste the molasses, we will have the actual experience of its sweetness. Similarly, if we practice meditation properly by following the correct path and receiving the proper instructions, we will experience the Dharma. In the *King of Samadhi* sutra it says that to meditate properly, one has to first receive instruction on meditation, and then one has to understand these instructions. There is a story of a *rishi,* a sage, who meditated for twelve years without achieving any real results. He died and was reborn a cat. The reason he was reborn a cat, not a human, was that he had not received the proper meditation instructions. Consequently, the Buddha said we must first listen to the teachings and then contemplate them before we meditate on them. He said that he himself had also listened to the teachings, contemplated them, and then meditated on them. As his followers, we should do the same.

PART I:
THE EIGHT CONSCIOUSNESSES

Chapter 2

The Mind as the Source of
Delusion and Nondelusion

3. There are those, who believe that the three realms and all beings,
Are a creation arising from themselves, or from another,
From both, or from no cause.
There are those who state that there is a creator:
Gampo-Cha, Shiva, Brahma, or Vishnu,
Or that there are external atoms,
Or truly existing imperceptible matter,
That has created the self and the world.

In the past there have been many different teachers from many
different traditions who have presented views on how to understand the nature of phenomena. They have taken views much different from Rangjung Dorje's view that external phenomena are
created by the mind. We need to understand why these teachings
are incorrect in order to have a clear understanding of how phenomena arise. Therefore Rangjung Dorje begins with a refutation
of inaccurate theories of how phenomena arise.

There are external appearances in the world and the beings
within it. The Buddhist tradition describes the world in terms of
three realms: the desire realm, the form realm, and the formless
realm.[10] Where did these realms come from? Some philosophical
schools state that things or phenomena originate from the self,
some state that things originate from other, some state things
originate from self and other, and some schools state that things
originate without any cause.[11]

13

The latter view was held by the Charvakas, a tradition that stated that the world had no cause whatsoever. They illustrated their view with the example that peas are round, but no one has rolled them into that shape; thorns are sharp, but no one has sharpened them. Similarly, they contended that the entire world occurs naturally, without any cause. Some other traditions believed that there was a creator who made this world. This is the view of the Bon religion, the religion that was already present in Tibet before the introduction of Buddhism in the seventh century. The Bonpos stated that "Fortune," or *Cha* in Tibetan, is the cause for the eventual attainment of prosperity and is also the creator of everything in the world.

In India there were three pre-Buddhist religions that believed in a creator: Shaivism, Brahmanism, and Vaishnavism. The Shaivites, followers of Shiva, believed that Shiva had a thought or dreamed, "this world is necessary," and that this thought created the world. The followers of Brahma believed that he gazed with his four faces into the four directions, and from this he created the entire world. The Vaishnavites believed that Vishnu, being very skillful and intelligent, created this world out of his own power.

It should be clear that nothing arises without a cause as claimed by the Charvakas. If this were the case, then there would be no point in planting seeds since there is no cause or reason for them to spout. If plants were created by Shiva or a god then there would be no point in planting seeds because the god would decide what to let grow. It is reasonable therefore to say that things are not created by gods, because all things need a cause.

Among the Buddhist schools there were different views on how outer phenomena were created. When the Buddha first began teaching, he gave teachings that were compatible to the understanding of his students. These became the Foundation vehicle teachings and were intended for *shravaka* practitioners. In these teachings, the Buddha said that there was no creator; instead everything was made up of minute atom-like particles. This was the view of the Vaibhashika school. Another Foundation vehicle teaching of the Buddha was that there were small invisible particles that were "hidden" from mind and from these the self and the external world were created. This was the view of the Sautrantika school. Although these two schools taught there is no creator, their views were still not completely correct.

WHAT THE BUDDHA TAUGHT

4. *The unique, Omniscient One taught that*
   Those three realms are purely mind.
   They are not derived from themselves, nor from that which is
      other,
   Not from both, nor from the absence of a cause.
   All phenomena arise through interdependence.
   They are, by their own nature, empty,
   Utterly free of being single or multiple,
   Utterly free of being falsehood or truth,
   Like the moon's reflection upon water and so on.
   Knowing this, the Buddha taught it to beings.

The Omniscient One (the Buddha) would teach according to the level of his students. He would often teach two different meanings: the definitive meaning and the provisional meaning. When the Buddha taught the definitive meaning, which describes the true nature of phenomena, he explicitly stated that all appearances in the three (the desire, the form, and the formless) realms are mind. In teaching the definitive meaning, the Buddha said that there was no external creator and that everything is created by, arises in, and is perceived by mind alone.

There were four major schools of Indian Buddhism: the Vaib-hashika, the Sautrantika, the Mind-only and the Middle-way schools. There are actually two different Mind-only schools: one that says that appearances are mind and nothing else, and the second that says that appearances were created by mind in the first place. This second school then taught that the three realms of existence—that is, all phenomena—did not arise due to a self or through others or through no cause at all; rather, it asserts that phenomena arise through interdependence or interdependent origination,[12] with one phenomenon dependent upon another, without a creator being involved.

A simple example of this is given in Kamalashila's *The Stages of Meditation*, which says that if one has a two-inch incense stick and a four-inch incense stick, the four-inch stick is clearly the longest, and this is agreed upon by everyone. But if one then adds a six-inch stick and takes away the two-inch stick, then suddenly the four-inch stick is the shorter stick. So being long or short, big or small, right or left, etc., always depends on the interdependence with other objects rather than the nature[13] or the inherent quality of the object itself. The incense stick is not short or long in itself; that quality occurs only through dependence upon other phenomena and through the analysis by the mind. Therefore the Chittamatra or Mind-only tradition taught that because of this, the mind alone is the basis for all appearances.

The mind is the source for everything, without a creator deity being necessary, because it is the mind that creates all actions, and therefore all karma. All happiness and unhappiness, anger, attachment, love, and compassion arise from the mind and nowhere else. So the mind is the source of all samsara and nirvana.

In a sutra the Buddha said, "Oh bodhisattvas, the three realms are only mind." That may make us think, "What about these houses, mountains, and fields that I see? They are all external to my mind!" However, when we see houses and fields in dreams, we think of them as being external objects that are not created by the mind, even though they are nothing other than projections of our mind. All that we see when we are awake is also nothing other than a creation of the mind.

We see objects such as houses, trees, and mountains on a gross level. In fact, when we look carefully, we realize that nothing exists as a single entity. Everything is actually made up of many components. For example, when we look at our hand, our mind conceives of it as a "hand." Actually, it is made up of skin, flesh, bones, and different fingers. When we examine the thumb more closely, we see it is composed of a nail, skin, and different joints, etc. There is really nothing to look at that can be considered even the thumb, yet our mind says "thumb." It is the same way for everything else: nothing exists as a single entity because it can always be broken down into smaller particles. Even if broken down to the smallest particle, we can analyze that particle and discover that this smallest particle has four sides—a north, south, west, and east. Therefore even the smallest particle cannot be defined as a singularity. Yet all these things seem like singularities in the conceptual formations of the mind. They arise in the mind; that is, they are mental constructions, and therefore their source is the mind.

HOW RANGJUNG DORJE GAINED REALIZATION

5. *From what source does this*
Delusion and non-delusion arise?
I have understood the nature of dependent origination,
In the same way that one sees one's own reflection in a mirror,
And knows that there is fire because there is smoke,
And I shall clearly describe it here.

Buddhists believe everything appears in the mind, just like an image appears in a mirror. Everything arises through dependent origination similar to a reflection in a mirror. For a reflection to occur one needs a visual image and also a mirror that reflects this image. It is the interdependence between the image and the mirror that allows us to see the image in the mirror. This example illustrates interdependence on the ultimate level.[14] Similarly, when we see smoke coming from a forest, we know that this is dependent upon fire; so when we see smoke, we know there is a fire there even if we cannot see the fire. This illustrates interdependence on the conventional level.

Rangjung Dorje gained knowledge and wisdom from listening to the teachings and the understanding that comes from contemplating them. Rangjung Dorje also received the actual practice instructions and teachings on the sutras and tantras from a guru in order to develop the understanding that comes from receiving the teachings. The sutras are the Buddha's Mahayana teachings and the tantras are the Buddha's Vajrayana teachings. He also received the teachings of the shastras, which are the commentaries on the Buddha's teachings. Rangjung Dorje received all these teachings and contemplated them. Having realized the essence of reality through study and contemplation, he experienced the source of samsara and nirvana. Therefore he was able to see this clearly, just like one sees one's reflection in a mirror.

17

Rangjung Dorje describes his realization in terms of the two truths. On the ultimate level, he realized the source of delusion and non-delusion; that is, the nature of phenomena. On the conventional level, he realized how phenomena arise through interdependence. Having attained these two realizations, he described the consciousnesses and wisdoms.

Chapter 3

All Appearances are the Mind

THE FIVE SENSORY CONSCIOUSNESSES

6. The five sensory consciousnesses create afflictions
Because of holding and rejecting
Forms, sounds, smells, tastes, and tactility.
What are these sensory objects?
If the wise examine well, they will know that
Nothing, such as atoms and so on, exists externally,
As anything other than cognition.

The five sensory consciousnesses of the eye, ear, nose, tongue, and body perceive the five sense objects of visual forms, sounds, tastes, smells, and body sensations. Basically, all sights, sounds, and smells are neither good nor bad, but some are perceived as being good and are accepted and some are perceived as bad and are rejected. These perceptions of pleasure and displeasure give rise to the afflictions or disturbing emotions (Skt. *kleshas*), which then cause all the suffering and illusory appearances of samsara.

   If those who are endowed with wisdom examine the cause of all this suffering and illusion carefully by wondering, "What are these sensory objects?" they then will discover that although thoughts of beauty and ugliness, good and bad, and so on, are associated with the sensory objects, these qualities are not actually inherent in the objects perceived. Instead these qualities come from the mind because there is no sensory object that exists independently outside that mind.

THE FOUR CONDITIONS FOR PERCEPTION TO OCCUR

There are four conditions necessary for a perception of an external object to result in a disturbing emotion. The first condition, called the "causal condition," is the condition where the ground (eighth) consciousness and the afflicted (seventh) consciousness have to be present.[15] The second condition, called the "primary condition," is the condition where the actual sensory faculty and its consciousness of the eye, the ear, the nose, the tongue, or the body must be present. The third condition, called the "objective condition," is the condition that the external sensory object such as a sight or sound or smell must be present. Without this sensory object the sensory consciousness cannot arise. For example, the ear consciousness will arise because of a sound the nose consciousness will arise because of a smell, and so on. So for these five sensory consciousnesses to arise there has to be an object that can be perceived by the sensory faculty. The fourth condition, called the "immediate condition," is the condition of the continuum of the mind. Since the mind is a succession of individual instants— there's a thought for one instant, then there's another thought the next instant—this continuum must also be present.

The result of these four conditions coming together is that we have a sensory experience that results in the perception of something which is either pleasant or unpleasant or neutral. If we perceive something as pleasant or beautiful, we think that it is good and we are pleased, and we then develop the disturbing emotion of desire or attachment. If we perceive something as unpleasant or ugly, we will dislike it, which will gradually develop into the disturbing emotion of aversion or anger. If we see something that we think of as neutral, we will not see the true nature of the object, and respond to it with the disturbing emotion of stupidity or ignorance. We can see from this that all the negative emotions come about as a result of perceiving an object that is automatically identified as good, bad, or neutral.

We experience happiness or unhappiness based on our perception. But even when we experience something as pleasant and enjoy it, we may later experience suffering from this same object. Happiness is impermanent and will eventually become a source of suffering because of loss of this desired event or object. This suffering then comes from the four conditions: the eight consciousnesses, the continuum of mind, the five senses, and their objects.

REFUTING THE ERRONEOUS VIEW THAT
THE SENSORY OBJECTS ARE NOT THE MIND

7. *If the substance of those sensory objects were other than consciousness,*
   They could not both be a single entity.
   A non-manifesting, immaterial awareness
   Does not create material substance.
   Therefore, a relationship where the latter arises from the former could not exist.
   With this view that sensory objects are other than consciousness,
   It will become illogical for sensory objects to appear from consciousness,
   Because they would have no connection.

Before explaining how all external phenomena are mind, Rangjung Dorje refutes the view held by many that external reality is not the mind. He uses the argument that if external phenomena were other than the mind, then external phenomena would have a different nature[16] than the mind. The view Rangjung Dorje is refuting here is the view that held that external phenomena are matter, and that the nature of consciousness is awareness.

If mind and external phenomena had completely different natures or essences, then there could be no connection or relationship between them, because objects wouldn't be able to arise out of the consciousness that perceived them. The only way that there could be a relationship between objects and their perceiver would be if they were to have the same nature, and then the objects would be able to arise out of the consciousness perceiving them. The relationship between matter and consciousness must be either between things of the same essence or between things of a different essence. An example of things having the same nature is like seeing an elephant in a dream; we see a dream elephant, and both the nature of

21

the elephant and the nature of the perceiver are mind. An example of two things having different natures is like seeing an elephant while waking. In this case, there must be an instant between the elephant and the consciousness perceiving it, because they cannot arise at exactly the same time; therefore, it is impossible for them to have a relationship other than cause and effect.

WHY EXTERNAL PHENOMENA ARE MIND[17]

8. *Therefore, all these various appearances,*
   Do not exist as sensory objects which are other than consciousness.
   Their arising is like the experience of self-knowledge.
   All appearances, from indivisible particles to vast forms, are mind.
   This means, that if nothing exists externally and separately,
   Brahma and the rest could not be creators.

When we learn that external objects are only mind and are not separately existing things, we might answer, "Well, I can see them. They are made out of matter, therefore, they are different from mind, which is not made up of matter but has the quality of clarity or awareness. So, mind and external objects are completely different things. One is solid matter and the other is clarity." To refute this argument we can use the previous example of a hand. We say, "Oh, I see a hand." But if we investigate more closely, we see a thumb, an index finger, a middle finger, a ring finger, and a little finger, skin, flesh, and bones. We then ask, "Where is this hand that I see?" In fact, the hand is just a conceptual fabrication. We then look at the thumb and say, "I see a thumb." But the thumb consists of the first, second, and third joints, and so on, and therefore also is made up of many different parts. We know that none of these parts are the thumb, and ask, "Well, where is the thumb?" There is only one answer: there is no actual thumb. We see something and think we see a hand, but in fact there is no real hand there. It is only a conceptual fabrication coming from the mind. The same analysis applies to the fingers, a mountain, a house, or to any other external object.

An explanation of the line in the verse that says, "Their arising is like the experience of self-knowledge" will be given next. We may hold the position that all external phenomena are composed of collections of real, minute particles and these indivisible particles are gathered together to make the external phenomena that we perceive. When we, however, examine these small particles more closely, we find that we cannot divide them into the smallest particle because each particle can be divided into still smaller particles. So there is no such thing as a particle that everything is made up of, and there is no reality in these external phenomena. So we must conclude that all external appearances arise from mind.[18]

We will never find an external object separate from our mind. We see things as being separate because, since the beginning of time, which we have spent in samsara, we have been habituated to the idea that phenomena exist externally. All external phenomena, from the smallest, indivisible particle to the largest mountain, appear from the mind alone. Many traditions say that the world and all beings inhabiting it were created by Brahma, Shiva, and Vishnu; they mistakenly assert that gods created the smallest particles, which we might call atoms. However, everything we experience, whether pleasant or unpleasant, arises from our mind through the power of our karma and is not created by gods.

EXPLANATION OF THE MENTAL CONSCIOUSNESS

9. *The relationship between the mental consciousness and mental*
   phenomena,
   Is like the experience of a dream.
   The mind focuses on phenomena
   And becomes attached to them.
   But they are devoid of any true reality.

Although we may intellectually agree with the statement that all objects are only experienced by mind and don't exist due to external causes, we do not actually believe this. We believe that there are two separate things: external objects and an inner consciousness perceiving them. Although we believe them to be separate, the Buddha taught that these events are not external but are only mind.

Ordinary logic disagrees with this. For example, if we were to say that this book that we are reading is our mind, we would think, "No, that is not true. The book was made by a printer and did not come from our mind; it is an external object." But when we dream, we also see external objects, yet none of them have an independent external existence; they are all just mental creations. In the same way, all external appearances that we perceive are created by our mind and do not have any independent existence.

The five sensory consciousnesses perceive sensory objects or events directly as mental images of visual forms, sounds, smells, tastes, and bodily feelings. These are then perceived by the sixth consciousness, which is the mental consciousness. The mental consciousness does not perceive the sensory objects directly, but as mental events. These mental images are sometimes termed *dharmas*, which is translated as "phenomena," meaning the purely mental phenomena that appear to the mind. The relationship between the mental consciousness and these mental phenomena is not direct, but rather like the experience in a dream. In a dream the mental phenomena appears to the sixth consciousness, which takes it as being real. A similar process occurs in a dream, in which all the appearances in the dream arise internally to the mind and are conceived of as being external phenomena. There is a strong attachment to these images being external phenomena, both in the dream and in waking.

The subject of Pramana describes mental consciousness as having two aspects: an external orientation and an internal orientation. The external orientation is when the mental consciousness becomes attached to the sensory form that is perceived by a sensory consciousness. For example when there is a sound, a mental consciousness engages that sound. This is the external orientation of the mental consciousness.

The mental consciousness with an internal orientation is called "self-knowledge," which is the mind being aware of itself. The Pramana tradition states that "One's own mind is not concealed from oneself." We have to ask someone else what they are thinking about, but we know exactly what we ourselves are thinking. This isn't because our mind is looking at itself as if it were something else. There is no dualism of something that is seen and something that is doing the seeing. We don't have to wonder, "What am I thinking?" because we can clearly perceive it. This internal orientation of the mental consciousness which looks[19] at the mind itself is called *rang rig*[20] in Tibetan, and means "self-knowing." Externally oriented mental consciousness is conceptual and inferential. When we look at something, for example, we can compare it with previous sights, we can analyze it to determine its qualities, and we can name it. In contrast, the internally oriented mental consciousness of looking at mind's own nature is nonconceptual and must be perceived directly. As ordinary (unenlightened) persons we can by inference understand that the mind is capable of seeing its own nature, but we do not have the direct experience or recognition of this self-knowledge. To recognize this self-knowledge directly, we have to engage in meditation to directly see the essence of mental consciousness. After we have done that, we should abide in this non-conceptual state.

If we do not recognize self-knowledge, but indulge in the externally oriented aspect of mental consciousness, then we will become involved in the usual flow of thoughts and remain in a state of delusion. But if we can reject the externally oriented consciousness and rest in self-knowledge, we will have effective meditation. Therefore it is taught, "Rest like an infant seeing a temple." When we bring a baby into a temple, the baby sees directly all the objects and images. It doesn't think, "Oh, that is a throne, that is the Buddha;" instead, the baby has a direct experience of the temple. During meditation, we should have this direct experience without thoughts and concepts and experience self-knowledge.

In terms of meditation, the important consciousness is the sixth. mental consciousness. When are doing a meditation involving visualization, some of us believe that we should see the visualization as clearly as in normal vision; however, in visualization we are using the mental consciousness, while in normal vision we are using a visual consciousness. Since a mental consciousness perceives the meaning of an object, it cannot perceive a clear picture in the way that the visual consciousness can. We cannot expect a visualization to be as clear as seeing an ordinary object. Also in tranquility (Skt. *shamatha*) and insight (Skt. *vipashyana*) meditation, we use the sixth consciousness. We are observing all the movements of thoughts in our mind. It is with the sixth consciousness that we are training in this meditation.

THE MIND IS EMPTY[21]

10. These six consciousnesses,
The appearances of sensory objects and of beings,
The attachment to a self, cognition
Whatever appearances are manifested
Are not created by anything which is other than themselves.
They are not created by themselves,
Nor created by both self and other,
Nor by the absence of both.

In the graduated path of meditation it is first taught that all external phenomena are mind. This has been covered in the previous chapter, and now we come to the discussion of how the mind itself, the six consciousnesses, has no inherent reality and is empty in nature. The verse begins by stating that there are no external appearances, only the internal six consciousnesses to which the external sensory objects, the belief in self, and the internal thoughts and feelings appear. These events or appearances are analyzed in the classic four-fold logic of Nagarjuna used in *The Perfection of Wisdom* (Skt. *Prajnaparamita*) teachings. These internal and external appearances are: (1) not created from themselves, (2) nor are they created from something outside themselves, (3) nor are they created from both themselves and other, (4) nor are they created from neither themselves nor other. In other words, they are empty by nature.

Rangjung Dorje now describes how all external things are mental manifestations. We may wonder if this is the same viewpoint as the Mind-only school, which asserts that all external phenomena are mental manifestations and that phenomena have no true existence. This school asserts that only the mind truly exists, which is why they are called the "Mind-only" school. Rangjung Dorje, however, goes further and teaches that the mind is birthless, has the quality of being empty, and possesses luminosity. The text shows that external things have no true existence, and when we investigate our mind, we discover that it also has no true existence. The usual example given is saying that a mountain defined as being "here" is different than a mountain over "there." But there is no definite "here" or "there" mountain, because the mountain over "there" becomes the mountain "here" when one goes across the valley. Therefore, mountains don't have an intrinsic nature of being here or there; everything is instead interdependent, with "here" depending on "there," and vice versa.

Similarly, the known and the knower also depend upon each other. When something is known, there is a knower; where there is a knower, something is known. If nothing were known, there would be no knower, because the knower depends on what is known for its existence. If external objects have no true existence, then the mind also has no true existence. If visual forms have no true reality, then visual consciousness has no reality; if sounds have no reality, then auditory consciousness has no reality and so on. If external phenomena have no true reality, then the six consciousnesses have no reality; if sense objects have no reality, then the actual senses themselves and the sense organs have no reality; if the sense organs have no reality, then the consciousnesses that arise from them have no reality. Therefore, if both external phenomena and internal consciousnesses have no true reality, then neither a self nor clinging to a self has true reality.

Even though there is nothing that inherently exists, things do obviously appear. We see a car and we open the door and climb in and drive along the highway. A vast variety of appearances do appear and do have an effect on us. We wouldn't, for example, deliberately drive our car into a wall. These appearances are part of relative or conventional reality, and they appear to mind because mind has luminosity. When this luminous aspect of mind, which is knowing awareness, is impure, we have consciousnesses. When this luminosity is pure, we have wisdom. Nevertheless, neither this luminosity nor this wisdom has any inherent reality on the ultimate level. Thus, all appearances come out of clarity or luminosity but have no inherent reality.

To summarize, it is said that external phenomena and inner consciousnesses are not created by:

(1) the self, (2) something other than the self, (3) both self and other, or (4) neither self nor other. Thus, all external phenomena and the inner consciousnesses experiencing this display have no true inherent existence.

THE SCRIPTURES ON THE EMPTINESS OF MIND

11. Therefore, as the Victorious One has taught,
All samsara and nirvana are just mind.

That all external phenomena are mind and that mind is empty can be proved through logic as this treatise has done. It can also be established by reading the scriptures of the Buddha. The Buddha taught that the mind is responsible for us attaining buddhahood and the mind is also responsible for us wandering in samsara. The Buddha has said that the mind is like an artist who paints whatever he wants. The mind uses the five mental aggregates of form, feeling, identification, formation, and consciousness to create whatever is perceived in the world.

Saraha (9th century CE) in India was one of the eighty-four *mahasiddhas* practicing the Mahamudra. He said that mind is the seed of everything. While we reside in our confused state in samsara, everything we experience comes from the mind, and when we achieve buddhahood, all the enlightened qualities and wisdoms also come from mind. Therefore, when we use our mind properly, we can obtain both the happiness of samsara and the happiness of nirvana. In this way the mind is like a wish-fulfilling jewel.[22]

Why is it that we are not always happy? It is that through countless lifetimes we have become thoroughly habituated to the false belief or delusion that external appearances are inherently existent or "real" and are distinctly separate from our mind.[23]

This process of how mind creates phenomena is elaborated in a sutra in which the bodhisattva Manjushri was asked by a deva,[24] "Has the external world not been created by someone?" and Manjushri replied, "Son of deva, the external world was not created by anyone. It was not created by Brahma, Shiva or someone else. The entire world was created through latent karmic imprints.[25] When these imprints developed and increased, they formed the earth, the stones, the mountains, and the seas. Everything was created through the development or propagation of these latent karmic potentials." Then the deva asked, "How can all external forms arise out of latent karmic imprints? All these mountains, oceans, the sun and moon are so solid and so vivid. How can they arise out of latent karmic imprints in the mind?" Manjushri replied, "These things arise through the power of development and the propagation of thought."

We have many examples of this in the East. For example, there was an old lady meditating on the visualization of herself being a tigress and she concentrated and focused so clearly that others actually saw her as an actual tigress. Also there is a well-known practice performed by monks to reduce their sexual desire by visualizing human bodies as containing all kinds of impure substances such as pus and urine. Sometimes other individuals can see these monks as having rotten and putrid bodies. While these two examples are small, occurring over brief periods of time, we can imagine how large objects such as mountains have been produced by the minds of millions and millions of sentient beings since beginningless time.

Table 2 The Transformation of Consciousnesses into Wisdoms

ORGAN	CONSCIOUSNESS	WISDOM	KAYA
Eye	1. Eye Consciousness	All Accomplishing Wisdom	Nirmanakaya
Ear	2. Ear Consciousness		
Nose	3. Nose Consciousness		
Tongue	4. Tongue Consciousness		
Body	5. Body Consciousness		
Mind	6A. Nonconceptual Mind Consciousness		
	6B. Conceptual Mind Consciousness	Dharmadhatu Wisdom	Svabhavikakaya
	7A. The Immediate Mind Consciousness	Discriminating Wisdom	Samboghakaya
	7B. Afflicted Mind Consciousness	Wisdom of Equality	
	8. The Ground Consciousness	Mirror-like Wisdom	Dharmakaya

Chapter 4

How the Eight Consciousnesses
Cause Delusion

The *Treatise Distinguishing Consciousness from Wisdom* presents an outline of the whole treatise in a brief form in the first eleven verses. We have reached the point in the treatise where each of these points is covered in more detail.

THE SUMMARY OF THE EIGHT CONSCIOUSNESSES

12. The causes, conditions, and interdependence,
*   Have been taught by the Buddha to be the six consciousnesses,*
*   The afflicted mental consciousness, and the ground consciousness.*

Causes, conditions, and interdependence are necessary for things to arise in the mind; they don't appear without a reason. For example, growing a flower requires a seed and the necessary conditions of water, sunlight, and soil. Finally, interdependence is necessary; the cause and conditions must be in the right amount and occur at the right time. If a flower has too much water or not enough sunlight, it will not grow. Likewise, birth in samsara doesn't just happen; its causes and conditions and their interdependence must be present for all the illusionary appearances of samsara to arise.

The six consciousnesses are literally called the "six accumulations," and resemble the teaching of the five skandhas. The six consciousnesses are not a single entity, are impermanent, and do not possess inherent reality; they are instead an accumulation of many moments of consciousness.

As an example of their impermanence, we assume that we have a single visual consciousness from morning to evening. Upon close examination, however, we discover that a visual consciousness only arises when a sensory object contacts the sensory organ. When this circumstance doesn't occur, the visual consciousness ceases. When we see a red color, a visual consciousness perceiving red arises and ceases. A visual consciousness arises for an instant and then ceases, allowing the next visual consciousness to arise and cease in the next instant. This process also applies to the other consciousnesses—an auditory consciousness perceives a loud sound and then a quiet sound and so on, with consciousnesses continually arising and ceasing in a succession of instants.

The samsaric appearances that arise from these causes and conditions are of two kinds: common and individual. Some appearances are the result of identical causes created by many beings, so that something will be seen by everyone in common, such as everyone in a particular room seeing that it has two pillars. However, there are certain individual causes and conditions that result in beings having their own individual experiences of happiness and discomfort. For example, some people taste chili and think it's delicious, while others taste it and experience discomfort. Even though the flavor and the sensory organs of their tongues are the same, differing individual experiences occur. These different perceptions are due to different latencies that have been laid down in the ground consciousness. The latencies of different individuals are different, thus making for different causes for the six sensory consciousnesses.

THE OBJECTIVE CONDITIONS OF THE CONSCIOUSNESSES

13. The six consciousnesses are dependent on objective conditions,
Which are the six sensory objects of form and so forth.

As previously mentioned, the arising of consciousness depends on four conditions: the objective condition, which is the sense-objects; the primary condition, which is the sense organs; the immediate condition, which is the immediate mentality that will be explained in conjunction with the seventh consciousness; and finally the causal condition, which is the eighth, ground consciousness. In more detail, the first condition is called the "object condition;" images, sounds, smells, tastes, and tactile sensations are perceived.

These make the five sensory objects, and the sixth object is the phenomena arising in the mental consciousness. The sixth, sensory object is called "phenomena" because the image appearing to the mind is not the actual direct perception of, for example, a visual form. A visual object is not directly perceived by the mind; rather, a conceptual image of the visual form appears. Similarly, when the mind conceives of a taste, there is no perception of the actual taste; instead, a concept of taste appears in the mind. None of the five objects are directly perceived by the mind. When an appearance of any one of the five objects arises in the mind, it becomes the sixth object. The six objects are the object conditions for the arising of the six consciousnesses.

These images alone would not be able to give rise to the six consciousnesses without the primary condition of the actual senses themselves—the sense of the eye, the sense of the nose, the sense of the ear, and so on.

The Primary Conditions of the Consciousnesses

14. Their primary conditions are the six sensory objects,
Which are clarity endowed with form.

The primary conditions or the main causes for perception are the sensory organs. These are often taken to be the eyes, the ears, the nose, the tongue, and the body. But these sensory faculties are not the actual physical sense organs themselves. Rather the Abhidharma, which describes the elements of mind in great detail, says that the senses are actually "the basis of the organs." As Rangjung Dorje says, "Which are clarity endowed with form." Clarity or luminosity is the faculty of knowing and shows the sense faculties have the power to perceive.[26] Jamgon Kongtrul explains the actual physical form of these faculties according to Tibetan medicine. The sensory faculty in the eye is said to be like a flax flower, which is blue in appearance. The sensory faculty of the nose is like a knot in white birch, like a hole, shaped similar to an ear. The sensory faculty of the ear is like a row of very fine copper needles. The sensory faculty of the tongue is like a moon split in half and laid on the tongue. The sensory faculty of the body is said to be smooth and permeates the entire body, except for the hair and nails.[27]

Thus the six consciousnesses arise as a result of the six sensory objects and six sense faculties; together, they add up to *the eighteen constituents of perception* (Skt. *ayatanas*), which are responsible for the appearances arising in the three realms.

THE SOURCE OF THE SIX CONSCIOUSNESSES

15. Both faculties and objects arise from the mind.
This manifestation of sensory objects and faculties
Is dependent upon an element that has been present
Throughout beginningless time.

The five noncognitive sensory consciousnesses perceive objects vividly because they do not discriminate between beautiful and ugly, desirable and undesirable, and so on. Nagarjuna compared these senses to an idiot who can see everything clearly, but cannot think, "this is good and that is bad." In contrast, the sixth, mental consciousness cannot directly perceive objects; it rather follows what is perceived by the sensory consciousnesses and has only a rough or vague idea of external forms. It is conceptual and conceives of phenomena as being good or bad, similar or different, and so on.

Having established that there are sensory objects and sensory faculties, we may now ask, "Where did these external phenomena come from?" The answer is that all external phenomena—houses, mountains, roads, and their perceptions—originated from the mind. They all arose out of the ground consciousness.

How is this possible? The answer lies in the fact that since beginningless time we have been perceiving sights, sounds, smells, tastes, and bodily sensations, and these perceptions have been creating imprints or latencies in the ground consciousness. Habituation of having experienced a certain visual form will create a latency for that very form. Eventually, that latency will manifest from the ground consciousness as a visual form again, but it will be perceived as external to ourselves.

34

Everything the mind thinks occurs within the mind itself. As mentioned before, the closest analogy of this process is a dream. Although dream phenomena have no connection to external objects, we become attached to their mental images which are, in fact, these imprints or latencies coming from the eighth consciousness. Because we think that dream phenomena and external objects are the same, we grasp at that thought. Apart from the grasping, there is no connection between phenomena experienced in mental consciousness and external objects. This is why it is said everything appearing to the five senses arises, in fact, only from mind.[28]

A BRIEF INTRODUCTION TO
THE SIXTH AND SEVENTH CONSCIOUSNESSES

16. *Though a sensory consciousness perceives an object*
Its particular characteristics are known by the mental event of
identification,
Which is dependent upon the mental consciousness:
The immediate mentality and the afflicted-mentality.

Briefly, we'll explain the Mind-only school associated with Asanga and the Madhyamaka or Middle-way school associated with Nagarjuna. The Mind-only followers state that all phenomena are mind; the Middle-way followers state that all phenomena are empty. This text presents the information in terms of experiential mahamudra meditation (in contrast to the methods of analytical meditation)[29] by first teaching that all phenomena are the mind and then describing the empty nature of the mind.

It is easier to first recognize that the nature of all phenomena is the mind; having gained that direct recognition, we realize that mind itself is empty. Presenting the subject in this order facilitates direct recognition, whereas simply learning the Madhyamaka view that phenomena are empty makes it difficult to gain understanding. Thus Rangjung Dorje first teaches that all phenomena are the mind and then teaches how the mind itself is birthless.

The sixth, mental consciousness has no form and is called the "intermediate consciousness" or the consciousness following immediately upon arising or immediately upon cessation. As soon as a sensory perception of form occurs, the mental conception of that form immediately arises. The other senses also have a mental conception immediately following perception. The sixth, mental consciousness, like the sensory consciousnesses, also exists in one instant and ceases in the next; mental consciousness that has ceased becomes the condition for the mental consciousness following in the next instant.

This verse introduces how the other consciousnesses fit in with the sensory consciousness in the process of perception. Even though the sensory consciousnesses perceive external sense objects, a thing is not recognized or perceived as a solid external object until this perceptual process reaches the mental consciousness and the object is identified. The mental consciousness, however, does not store a memory of all the objects—this comes from the seventh and eighth consciousnesses. The seventh consciousness is particularly mentioned, and it has two aspects or functions: it serves as the immediate mentality, which ensures for the continuity of the mind, and it is also responsible for the afflicted mentality of a continual belief in "I," which is responsible for generating the disturbing emotions.

THE IMMEDIATE ASPECT
OF THE SEVENTH CONSCIOUSNESS

17. The first of those is immediate because
It is the condition for the arising and ceasing of the six
consciousnesses.
It occurs in the same numbers as those of
The momentary arising and ceasing of the six consciousnesses.
It can be known by a mind that is yoga-endowed
And through the teachings of the Victorious One.

The third of the four conditions needed for perception to occur is called the "immediate condition." When we consider both the afflicted and the immediate aspects of the seventh consciousness, we must know that they are always present within the six consciousnesses. The instant a visual object is seen, for example, the visual consciousness ceases, allowing the next instant of consciousness to arise. This sequence applies to all six consciousnesses. The immediate mind is the condition for the immediate arising and cessation of the six consciousnesses; when a consciousness ceases, it does not disappear, instead it subsides into the ground consciousness. The immediate mentality is the condition for all appearances to arise from any of the consciousnesses and to settle into the ground consciousness.

How does the immediate mentality cause instants of the mind to arise? An instant of mind cannot arise if there isn't a preceding instant of mind that ceases. There has to be a continuum of instants that immediately follow the preceding instants. When one instant of mind ceases, a latency in the ground consciousness immediately manifests as the next instant of mind. This power of immediacy never ceases. It is continually present so that the continuity of the mind is never interrupted.

How can we know this to be true? This can be seen by the "yoga-endowed." The word *yoga* is Sanskrit for "union" and in this context refers to the union of tranquility and insight meditation. By directly seeing our mind with shamatha and vipashyana meditation, we can see the immediate mind. We see how the arising of the six consciousnesses themselves is also a precondition for the arising of the six consciousnesses—because of the immediate consciousness, an instant of consciousness settles into the ground consciousness as soon as it ceases. The other method of gaining this knowledge is by understanding the Victorious One's (the Buddha's) teachings. We are able to understand that the immediate mind arises on account of there being a condition for the six consciousnesses and that it is also a condition for their arising.

It has been explained how all phenomena arise from the mind and how the mind itself is empty. With everything in samsara and nirvana appearing from the mind, we discover that the mind itself manifests as the eight consciousnesses. We all experience phenomena differently; for example, two people can go to the same movie and one will love it and the other will hate it. Also, beings in the six different realms experience phenomena differently. Hungry ghosts, for example, will perceive all kinds of desirable things and will also perceive that they can't obtain them.[30] All experiences, whether happiness or suffering, are due to particular causes and conditions. The basic cause of these experiences is the eighth, ground consciousness, the *alaya* consciousness. We can begin to understand the function of the ground consciousness through our daily experience. We have a basic clarity of the mind, which is an awareness or a continuous knowing. When we look, hear, think, and so on, there is always a continuity of the mind—a knowing that accompanies us from birth until death—with the continuum of this clarity present until we achieve buddhahood. Every action we take creates a latent karmic imprint, and these tendencies automatically flow into the ground consciousness where they are stored. These karmic imprints do not, however, remain stored, because they manifest sooner or later. These become our experience of samsara.

THE AFFLICTED ASPECT OF THE SEVENTH CONSCIOUSNESS

18. The second is an aspect of this immediate mentality.
It is called the 'afflicted-mentality' because
It believes the mind as self, possesses pride,
Has attachment to the self, and has ignorance,
And gives rise to all the destructive views.

After the six consciousnesses are described, the text commences explaining the seventh consciousness. This consciousness is afflicted and immediate. The seventh consciousness is the ever-present feeling of "I" or "self," the basis of ego. Because the mind is bound by this consciousness, it is called "afflicted." The feeling of "I" is present in one instant and when that instant ceases, it is present in the next instant. That is why it is called the "immediate consciousness." There is never a discontinuity in the mental continuum; as long as there is a mind, there is a continuous succession of instants immediately preceding each other. We cannot say that this succession of instants stops even after a hundred years. There is the continuous succession of instants of consciousness, and this is called the "immediate consciousness."

The seventh, afflicted consciousness is also present in all beings as a very subtle clinging to a self, which is often explained in terms of mind and mental events.[31] Mind and mental events refer to the clarity and awareness of the mind, which sees the nature of things. Mind is the basic awareness and includes all the consciousnesses.

When the mind changes, a mental event arises. There are fifty-one mental events listed in the Abhidharma. A mental event denotes that the mind has undergone a change—aspiration gradually becomes *samadhi*, which is positive, and feelings of resentment may become deceit, which is negative.

The afflicted mind (also called the "klesha-consciousness") is described in terms of four mental events: (1) clinging to a self by thinking there is a "me" and an "I;" (2) pride, which is believing the "I" is superior; (3) attachment to the self, which is believing oneself more deserving than others; (4) and ignorance, which accompanies the above three and is ignoring how things truly are (i.e., the egolessness of self). We may wonder whether the afflicted mind is good or bad. Generally, there are three types of actions or karma: good actions done with the motivation to help others, negative actions done with the motivation to harm others, and neutral actions such as walking, eating, or sitting, which have neither a good or bad motivation. There are two kinds of neutral actions: those that do not obscure liberation, and those that do. Walking somewhere does not cause obscurations or prevent liberation, whereas clinging to a self does prevent liberation and so is an obstacle. Yet it is in itself not good or bad, because if we think something like, "Oh, I must do good actions and need to accumulate merit," subsequent actions are good; or conversely, "Oh, I have to do something bad," the subsequent action becomes negative.

Rangjung Dorje presents a fairly unique view of the seventh consciousness. Generally, what was taught by the Buddha in the Mahayana teachings is called the sutras, and the Buddha's instructions on meditational deities and Vajrayana practice are called the tantras. When the Buddha's teachings were translated into Tibetan, they were placed in a collection called the Kangyur. There are two sections to the Kangyur: one dealing with the sutras and one dealing with the tantras. The Third Karmapa used both the sutras and the tantras for this text, instead of just the sutras. His description of how the eighth consciousness stores karmic imprints is clarified in a tantra called *The Tantra of the Vajra's Point*, which deals with how the mind perceives external phenomena. In the sutras of the Kangyur, the Mind-only followers, in their teaching on the eight consciousnesses, taught that the seventh consciousness is only an afflicted consciousness underlying a continuous belief in a self but is not involved in the immediate condition. Rangjung Dorje's own special view, however, combines the sutra and tantra views and adds the Middle-way view to the Mind-only view, so that here the seventh consciousness is taught to have the aspect of immediate mentality as well as afflicted mentality.

CHARACTERISTICS OF THE IMMEDIATE AND AFFLICTED MENTALITIES

19. The immediate mentality, which is instantaneous
Upon the cessation of the six consciousnesses,
Is the location for the arising of those consciousnesses.
The afflicted mentality is the location for the afflictions.
Therefore, mentality has two aspects
Due to their power to create, and its power to obscure.

Another way to look at mind is to consider it as a succession of instants rather than a single entity. The moment an instant of consciousness arises, it ceases, allowing the next instant of consciousness to arise. Within this progressive succession of instants, external objects are perceived. We may think that the presence of an external object causes sensory consciousnesses to arise and therefore that an external object is the causal condition and that the sensory consciousnesses are its effect. However, if an object were the cause and the consciousness were its result, then what would happen when the instant passed?[32] If we perceive the effect, then the cause must have ceased; thus, the object would have ceased. If a consciousness were the result in the following instant of consciousness, and its cause had existed in the previous instant, then the consciousness (the effect) would not be present when the object is present (the cause). They would not be connected and therefore have no relationship; thus, one cannot be the cause and the other the effect. We may claim that they exist at the same time, in a cause and effect relationship. Yet if they existed simultaneously, there would be no need for a cause because its effect would already be present. Therefore, it is not logical to claim that an external object is the cause for a sensory consciousness of that object.

Non-Buddhists and Foundation vehicle Buddhists say that the mind and external objects are different. However, if we carefully analyze the situation, we discover that external objects and inner mind are one. External objects actually arise from the mind, just like a dream. In a dream we see forms, but there are no forms that exist outside of our mind. In a dream we see, hear, smell, taste, and feel bodily sensations, but there are no sounds, smells, tastes, or sensations existing outside our mind. Yet they do have appearance—an unreal appearance. Similarly, while waking, everything we see is an appearance and arises from our mind.

Finally, Rangjung Dorje summarizes the two main functions of the afflicted consciousness. The afflicted consciousness is the source or "location" for the arising negative emotions or afflictions. This continuously present belief in a self gives rise to desire, anger, ignorance, envy, pride, and so on. This verse then concludes that the seventh consciousness has two aspects: the power to create the six consciousnesses (the immediate aspect) and the power to obscure (the afflicted aspect), which prevents the attainment of liberation.

THE GROUND CONSCIOUSNESS

20. *To those with superior understanding,*
 The Buddha taught the 'ground consciousness.'
 It was also named the 'foundation consciousnesses,'
 The 'location consciousness,' and the 'acquiring consciousness.'
 All the actions created by the other seven consciousnesses
 Are accumulated distinctly and impartially within it,
 Like rain and rivers flowing into the ocean.
 Therefore it is also named the 'ripening consciousness.'

The first two levels of this verse are a brief explanation of the eighth, ground consciousness and the rest of the lines are the detailed description of this consciousness.

The fourth of the four conditions for perception to occur is the causal condition, or the ground consciousness. The ground or *alaya* consciousness was not mentioned in the Foundation or Theravada texts, which describe only the first six consciousnesses.

The seventh and eighth consciousnesses were not taught in the Buddha's early teachings because they could have incorrectly been taken for being permanent and therefore the same as the belief in a permanent self (Skt. *atman*). However, the ground consciousness is not a permanent self, because its nature is emptiness. It is the source of all samsaric appearances. A self is considered basic, and we have great attachment to it, but this isn't true for the ground consciousness. In the Abhidharma teachings, however, the Buddha said, "I have explained the ground consciousness to those who are pure," meaning that the ground consciousness was introduced to Mahayana bodhisattvas or "those with superior understanding" in this verse.

The ground consciousness has many functions, so Rangjung Dorje explains these by giving each of them names. These are called the "basis consciousness" because the eighth consciousness is the basis for the mind; the "location consciousness" because it is the location of the mind; and the "acquisition consciousness" because it acquires all the karmic latencies that are laid down.

The reason the Buddha taught the subject of the ground consciousness at all is that when karma accumulates, the latent karmic imprints settle in the ground consciousness to express themselves at a later time. A karmic latency will awaken as experiences of suffering or happiness. Positive karma doesn't immediately express itself as happiness; so doing many positive deeds will not result in a rebirth in a paradise. Rather, the karmic latencies rest within the ground consciousness and arise later as a result; for example, the joy of being reborn in a slightly more favorable situation. Similarly, accumulated negative karma does not express itself immediately as rebirth in the hell realms, but the karmic imprints remain in the ground consciousness to ripen under the appropriate circumstances, causing suffering later on. Thus the ground consciousness can be said to be the "ripening consciousness."

The negative and the positive qualities increase due to habituation. For example, a person becomes angry again and again and then becomes habituated to anger, causing the latency of anger to increase in the mind. The same is true with desire. When one desires something again and again, the latencies of desire increase. This process also occurs for the positive qualities: a person may not have much love, compassion, or wisdom, but by engaging in love, compassion, or study, the imprints of these positive qualities increase in the ground consciousness. If there were only six consciousnesses, then thoughts would arise and cease without anything left to increase or develop (such as the good qualities to reach buddhahood). The increase of these positive qualities occurs only because positive tendencies are planted in the ground consciousness.

The ground consciousness is the foundation and location for the mind because all karmic latencies are stored in the ground consciousness. A momentary visual consciousness instantly ceases when the next instant appears and does not occur again; instead a new momentary visual consciousness appears. Similarly, a mental consciousness is created and ceases instantly; sometimes a mental consciousness does not appear at all. However, the latencies for the arising of these consciousnesses are contained within the ground consciousness. Thus, we can remember a visual perception that occurred in the past, and remembering it strengthens the latency.

The ground consciousness is very important for our practice of the Dharma. If we do not maintain mindfulness and awareness, our disturbing emotions gradually increase, from day to day, from lifetime to lifetime. However, if we develop mindfulness and awareness, our mind will gradually improve due to the latencies being established in the ground consciousness. For example, when we begin to practice, there may not be much love and compassion in our meditation. But if we persist and meditate on love and compassion, through the gradual accumulation of the latencies of love and compassion in the ground consciousness we will gradually progress to a point where our meditation will have vast love and compassion.

In terms of Dharma practice the ground consciousness is very important, because through meditation our mind overcomes negativity and develops positive imprints. Habituating ourselves to positive thoughts and actions allows negative imprints to decrease and positive qualities to increase. Meditation is very similar to habituation.[33] By developing samadhi, negative tendencies can be transformed into positive imprints, which can be developed until buddhahood is attained.

We can witness the effect of latencies in our daily life. Some children are very intelligent and some are not. This is due to the presence or absence of latencies in previous lifetimes. Some children are naturally very kind due to positive latencies laid down in their ground consciousnesses in previous lifetimes, and some children are very aggressive due to negative latencies. We can also see an aggressive child who has bad behavior gradually change as he grows older; through his cultivation of mindfulness and awareness, he can slowly, with the right training, establish new latencies by developing love, compassion, and humility as an adult. Conversely, some good children grow up to be bad due to the negative latencies they establish during their childhood.

The eighth consciousness is also the foundation of experience. Should someone be born into a higher existence of a god, jealous god, or human being, his or her experiences of happiness would be based upon the ground consciousness; and should someone fall into the lower realms, his or her experiences would also be based on the ground consciousness. Thus the eighth consciousness is the basis of all experiences within samsara, including future experiences. Creating imprints in the present leads to experiencing their results in the future; like a child who goes to school and studies hard—that activity will create an imprint in the child's mind that will allow him or her to become a teacher later on. If there were no learning, there would be no imprint and no possibility of being a teacher in the future. This is how the eighth consciousness functions and why it is responsible for the various existences in samsara and why it is also called the "consciousness of acquisition."

The five sensory and the sixth, mental consciousnesses are positive, negative, or neutral. The seventh, afflicted consciousness is neutral but has two possibilities: it may be ignorant and therefore the basis of the disturbing emotions, and it may be obscuring because it obscures liberation. The eighth, ground consciousness is also neutral, but it is not obscuring like the afflicted consciousness; it instead has an aspect of clarity. This luminosity allows all phenomena (places, bodies, existences, and so forth) to manifest, but does not obscure liberation.

The other seven consciousnesses create positive and negative imprints in the eighth consciousness. A simile to how this occurs is given in the text: when it rains, the water naturally flows into the rivers, and the rivers, whether they are dirty or clean, naturally flow into the ocean. Similarly, positive and negative imprints naturally flow into the ground consciousness.

> 21. *As it creates everything,*
>   *And is the ground from which all seeds sprout,*
>   *It is described as the 'causal condition.'*
>   *However, because it is eliminated*
>   *When the seven consciousnesses are negated,*
>   *It is also called the 'conditional consciousness.'*

All the karmic seeds, good or bad, within the ground consciousness sprout and manifest as the other seven consciousnesses, as if the ground consciousness were the ocean and the other seven consciousnesses were waves that appear upon its surface. The ground consciousness is responsible for all illusory appearances, but is not the basis of buddhahood, which is freedom from delusion. This is why the eighth consciousness is a consciousness and not a wisdom.

This concludes the section of the treatise that deals with the impure states of mind, the consciousnesses. The ground consciousness is the source of all delusory experiences. It is not the basis of buddhahood, because buddhahood is freedom from delusion. The nature of the ground consciousness is delusion; it is not in harmony with the true nature of reality. When buddhahood or *arhatship* is attained, the ground consciousness is transformed. When the ground consciousness ceases, all the consciousnesses are transformed into ultimate wisdom.

To summarize, there are impure consciousnesses and pure wisdoms. In defining the impure consciousnesses, it has been taught that the root of samsara and nirvana is the mind and that the mind itself is birthless.

Table 3
The Five Paths

1. Path of Accumulation	**Practices** mindfulness, recognizes the four marks of existence (impermanence, absence of a self, suffering, and emptiness) **Practices** four renunciations, **Practices** four concentrative absorptions (strong interest, perseverance, attentiveness, and investigation)
2. Path of Application	**Practices** five controlling powers (confidence, sustained effort, mindfulness, samadhi, and prajna). These powers become "unshakable" at the end of this path.
3. Path of Seeing (Insight)	**Attains** the first bodhisattva level of perceiving emptiness. **Develops** true awareness of the Four Noble Truths and their 16 aspects. **Develops** the seven factors of enlightenment (memory, investigation of meaning and values, effort, joy, refinement and serenity, samadhi, equanimity).
4. Path of Cultivation	**One** goes through the 2nd to 10th bodhisattva levels. **One** practices the eight-fold Noble Path (right view, right intention, right speech, right action, right livelihood, right effort, right mindfulness, and right meditation).
5. Path of Fulfillment	**This** is Buddhahood.

PART II
THE FIVE WISDOMS

Chapter 5

The Transformation of the Consciousnesses into the Wisdoms

THE FIVE WISDOMS AND THE THREE KAYAS

Jamgon Kongtrul has written a commentary on this text called *The Adornment of Rangjung Dorje's View.* At this point Jamgon Kongtrul has added information on how the five aggregates are transformed into wisdoms at the time of buddhahood. Although this does not appear in Rangjung Dorje's treatise, it will be helpful to discuss it here.

The five aggregates (Skt. *skandhas*) literally mean "heaps" and are form, sensation, perception, formation, and consciousness. Each of these aggregates is transformed upon reaching enlightenment. The aggregate of sensation (which includes within itself the three kinds of suffering: the suffering of suffering, the suffering of change, and the all-pervasive suffering) transforms into freedom from suffering as well as an unbroken continuity of great bliss. The aggregate of perception is transformed into the unhindered ability to teach the Dharma. The aggregate of formation is transformed into miraculous deeds and the gathering of Dharma students. Finally, the aggregates of consciousnesses are transformed into the five wisdoms. As may be seen it is the sixth, mental consciousness that is the aspect of mind that becomes the wisdoms at the level of enlightenment.

Jamgon Kongtrul describes four causes within the practice of the path of Dharma that give rise to four of the five wisdoms. Hearing and contemplating the full range of the Buddha's teachings in the Tripitaka (the Vinaya, the Sutras, and the Abhidharma) will cause "mirror-like wisdom" to develop. Engaging in the meditation of helping all sentient beings without any partiality to friends

49

or aversion to enemies will cause the "wisdom of equality." The giving of Dharma teachings with the motivation of love and compassion and a desire to help all sentient beings will cause "discriminating wisdom" to develop. Finally, the accomplishing of activities to benefit others is the cause for "all-accomplishing wisdom." We could add that the realization of the true nature of phenomena is the cause for the fifth, "dharmadhatu wisdom."

There are three realms (Skt. *kayas*). There is the *dharmakaya*, which is the pure realm of complete enlightenment. This manifests as the *sambhogakaya*, which is a pure realm where only realized beings (bodhisattvas and buddhas) can visit and receive teachings. Finally, there is the *nirmanakaya*, which is our earthly realm, inhabited by beings in samsara.

By diligently listening to and contemplating the Dharma and meditating on it, we are able to slowly eliminate the disturbing emotions and gradually develop the wisdom of the true nature of phenomena. We progress through the ten bodhisattva levels terminating in the attainment of buddhahood. At this point we have completely eliminated the causes of samsara: negative karma and the disturbing emotions. Our suffering is replaced with the experience of great bliss and peace. This is the first benefit of buddhahood, which principally liberates oneself. Upon attaining buddhahood we also eliminate all obstacles to our wisdom and attain perfect realization, or "omniscience." This benefits others because with this knowledge we can show them how they too can attain buddhahood. This complete elimination of the disturbing emotions and the cognitive obstructions is the Buddha's "dharmakaya" or "the body of the Dharma." This elimination of emotional and cognitive obstacles is illustrated by the Tibetan name for the "Buddha," which is *sang gye*. The first syllable *sang* denotes the Buddha has eliminated all defilements, and the second syllable *gye* denotes the Buddha has full realization.

The dharmakaya is principally an emanation of the Buddha's mind and has three qualities to help sentient beings. The dharmakaya has the quality of complete wisdom, it manifests compassion for all beings, and it has the power to provide refuge for them.

The dharmakaya is divided into two kayas or bodies: the dharmakaya and the *svabhavikakaya*. The aspect of the dharmakaya that is the wisdom of the variety of phenomena (Tib. *ji nye pa*) is called the "dharmakaya". The aspect of the dharmakaya that is the wisdom of the true nature of phenomena (Tib. *ji ta ba*) is the "svabhavikakaya." Under this system, the realms become four.

The clarity of the dharmakaya's wisdom is called "the mirror-like wisdom." All images, whether a king's castle or rotting meat, appear clearly as in a mirror. But while clearly seen, there is no attachment to these appearances. The Buddha is able to clearly see human beings' purity and impurities, their delusions and suffering. Due to mirror-like wisdom, everything is precisely known by the Buddha. Whatever is reflected in the mirror of this wisdom appears unmistakably; that is, white does not appear as yellow and yellow does not appear as red. Similarly, the dharmakaya perceives everything as it really is.

The sambhogakaya comes from the Sanskrit word *kaya*, which literally means "body," and *sambhoga*, meaning "enjoyment." The Sanskrit word refers to the spreading of the Buddha's activity among those interested in receiving teachings. Usually, enjoyment has the connotation of receiving wealth and pleasure, but that is not the enjoyment of a buddha. Enjoyment in this context refers to buddha activity bringing all bodhisattvas to the state of buddhahood. Through the Buddha's activity, the bodhisattvas are endowed with enjoyment.

The sambhogakaya has two wisdoms. First is the wisdom of equanimity, in which everything is seen impartially. With this wisdom there is no distinction between important and unimportant, self and other, best or worst; nevertheless, this does not mean that a buddha cannot discern good and bad, suffering and bliss, delusion and non-delusion. The sambhogakaya can discriminate between these, because the sambhogakaya has the second wisdom, discriminating awareness; phenomena are distinguished accurately, but are viewed impartially.

Impure beings that have no aspiration to receive Dharma teachings and have various dispositions and interests also exist. That is why buddhas manifest in different ways. In the sutras it is written that some persons enter the path by encountering a buddha's body—a buddha in a form body. Some persons enter the path upon hearing a buddha's teachings, such as Shakyamuni's student Shariputra who completely understood his teachings by just hearing them. Others enter the path upon seeing miracles, so the

Buddha sent persons like Maudgalyana[34] to perform miracles. Yet others enter the path by observing the Buddha's behavior, such as Shakyamuni's pupil Upali who was impressed by the Buddha's perfect behavior of dressing properly, walking with discipline, and so on. The nirmanakaya also has the wisdom of all-accomplishing actions.

The Buddha, being completely free of delusion, can correctly teach other beings and free them from delusions so that they also will be able to see the true nature of things. The wisdom that sees the true nature of phenomena is the "dharmadhatu wisdom" and belongs to the svabhavikakaya.

THE TRANSFORMATION OF THE GROUND CONSCIOUSNESS[35]

22. This ground consciousness,
   Which is the identity of everything external and internal,
   Is the source of everything that should be eliminated.
   It has been taught that it will be overcome
   By the 'vajra-samadhi.'

We now return to the root text, which begins this second section on the five wisdoms with an explanation of the transformation of the ground consciousness into the five wisdoms.

As mentioned before, Rangjung Dorje uses a Mahamudra view of the ground consciousness which is a little different from how it is traditionally presented by the Mind-only followers, who held that the ground consciousness is truly existent and is the source of samsara and nirvana. If the ground consciousness were the source of nirvana, then we would have to conclude that the ground consciousness continues after the attainment of buddhahood. However, in this treatise the ground consciousness is said to be completely empty and the foundation from which all the delusions of samsara appear. It is the storehouse containing all the latencies of samsaric appearance. Although its nature is neutral and it does not impede liberation in itself, it is the source of everything that has to be eliminated. This suggests that the ground consciousness is the foundation for samsara, but not for nirvana. When the ground consciousness is eliminated by "the vajra samadhi"—with *vajra* meaning something which is "indestructible" and *samadhi* meaning "meditation"—it is transformed into the wisdoms and is no longer the ground consciousness. So the nature of the ground consciousness is delusion, not the true nature of reality. When buddhahood or arhatship is attained, the ground consciousness ends.

The ground consciousness is the true identity of external phenomena such as mountains and internal phenomena such as thoughts. This is because the ground consciousness is the source of all the illusory appearances of samsara. Although its nature is neutral and it does not impede liberation in itself, it is the source of everything that has to be eliminated.

MIRROR-LIKE WISDOM[36]

> 23. *When the ground consciousness, with its obscurations, is*
> *negated*
> *At that time, there will be the 'mirror wisdom.'*
> *All wisdoms appear in it, without the concept of 'mine.'*
> *It is uncircumscribed and eternally possessed.*
> *It realizes all that is to be known,*
> *without being directed towards them.*
> *It is described as 'the dharmakaya,'*
> *Because it is the foundation for all the wisdoms.*

The first wisdom is the mirror-like wisdom, which is the wisdom of the dharmakaya. The eight consciousnesses are transformed into the five wisdoms when a person is about to become a buddha. At this boundary, there is a final trace of the ground consciousness left that is eliminated by the vajra-like samadhi and buddhahood is achieved, transforming the ground consciousness into mirror-like wisdom.

Since mirror-like wisdom itself is freedom from delusions, it sees the delusions, experiences, aspirations, and interests of others as clearly as if they were reflected in a mirror. Ordinarily, we can see only what is in front of us, but mirror-like wisdom enables us to see everything in all directions, without any mistakes at all, and it leads to great understanding because all aspects are seen so clearly.

From the clarity or luminosity of the ground consciousness, external phenomena seem to be really there, as if they were external objects. The ground consciousness also gives rise to internal phenomena of our mind being seen as the self, resulting in the development of the mind poisons such as attachment and anger. All these phenomena that come from the ground consciousness appear very vividly to us. When the ground consciousness has been transformed into mirror-like wisdom, there aren't any more clear or vivid delusions or appearances of samsara; clarity becomes this mirror-like wisdom. We may wonder if the elimination of the ground consciousness results in an emptiness such as a vacuum of empty space. But since it isn't like that, this state is described as a mirror in which a reflection appears vividly, without any sense of self. There is no grasping at the thought of "I" or "me;" everything just appears clearly.

A wisdom may be permanent or changing. For example, the wisdom of all-accomplishing actions undergoes changes depending on the needs of sentient beings, whereas the mirror-like wisdom is changeless, continuously present, and permanent, like the ground consciousness. Anything, whether beneficial or harmful, will appear to the mirror-like wisdom clearly, continuously, and impartially without any distinction between self and other.

Mirror-like wisdom is the wisdom of love and compassion; it gives rise to compassion, and that compassion gives rise to power. Unlike the ground consciousness, which is the root of all the illusory appearances of samsara, mirror-like wisdom is the source of the five wisdoms and is called the *dharmakaya* (Tib. *chö kyi ku*). The Sanskrit word *kaya* means "body" or "aspect," and the word *dharma* comes from the Sanskrit *dru dhrina*, meaning "to hold;" thus, *dharma* means "to hold" something so it doesn't fall down. So *dharma* means things are prevented from falling down into samsara or lower existences. The word *dharma* was translated into Tibetan as *chö*, which means "to repair, correct, or heal." For example, if an error were to occur, we would correct it; the Tibetan word for correcting something is *chö*. It is also used to heal an illness, and to describe situations where everything is going well or prospering—where all the good qualities are being developed and all the negative things are being eliminated.

THE WISDOM OF EQUALITY

24. The 'afflicted mentality'
Is utterly defeated by the 'fearless samadhi.'
The kleshas are utterly eliminated on
the paths of insight and meditation.
The subsequent absence of afflictions,
The absence of samsara and nirvana,
Is described as the 'wisdom of equality.'

The second wisdom is the wisdom of equality or equanimity, which is the result of the seventh, afflicted consciousness having been transformed. The afflicted consciousness possesses subtle ego-clinging until it is transformed and there is no longer a distinction between self and other or the thought of "I" and "mine." This transformation occurs at the eighth bodhisattva level and is attained through the samadhi of fearlessness whose courage is compared to that of a lion—an animal that cannot be defeated by any of the other animals.

This courageous samadhi or meditation overcomes the afflicted mentality of the seventh consciousness. When we are thus afflicted by clinging to a belief in a self, everything becomes frightening, and we become cowards. Even if a little stone is flicked at us, we instinctively react in fear. This is because we are clinging to a self and are afraid of the self being harmed. This courageous meditation enables us to overcome the afflicted mentality and not be afraid of anything or anyone.

Until the eighth bodhisattva level, we engage in samadhi that still has some disturbing emotions or kleshas present. Sometimes the samadhi is stable; at other times the disturbing emotions arise and must be eliminated. In any case, they are completely pacified on the eighth bodhisattva level.

Different kinds of disturbing emotions are eliminated on the five paths of meditation. On the first two paths, those of accumulation and junction, disturbing emotions become controlled and are overcome, but their seeds are still present. Consequently, the second path is one of aspiration—the aspiration to eliminate the disturbing emotions. On the third path, that of insight, the true nature of phenomena is realized, but it is not enough to eradicate the poisons, because we need to become familiarized with prevailing insight and meditate to intensify the tendency of seeing the true nature of phenomena. On the fourth path, that of meditation, we habituate ourselves to that insight.

The obvious and coarse disturbing emotions are vanquished when the true nature of phenomena is first seen. The subtle disturbing emotions, however, are not eliminated until the path of meditation. For example, when we see something we are attracted to, attachment and craving arise; when attachment and craving have been eliminated, everything is seen impartially, with an understanding of the equality of all things. This also applies to anger, because anger implies wanting to get rid of the unpleasant. Eliminating the resulting aggression allows everything to be seen impartially. Similarly, pride creates a biased opinion, and when it is eliminated, all beings are considered impartially. Ignorance is partial understanding and is of two types—mixed and unmixed. Mixed ignorance arises with desire, anger, and pride; when it is eliminated, everything is understood equally, and a state of equality and peace are established.

There is the gradual elimination of the disturbing emotions beginning on the path of seeing and lasting throughout the path of meditation. The disturbing emotions gradually decrease and the wisdoms gradually increase. When the afflicted consciousness is completely vanquished on the eighth bodhisattva level, then the last disturbing emotion ends and the complete wisdom of equality is attained.

Not only is the afflicted mentality eliminated, but also the disturbing emotions are eliminated by the third path of insight and the fourth path of meditation, which correspond to the tenth bodhisattva level. The conceptual aspects of the afflicted consciousness are eliminated by seeing the true nature of phenomena, while the subtle, inherent aspects are eliminated by meditation.

As long as there are disturbing emotions and attachment to a self, there is a division into good and bad, self and other, resulting in many different kinds of suffering. For example, one thinks oneself better than others, so pride develops, or one thinks that others are doing better than oneself, so envy and jealousy develop.

When the afflictions are eliminated, the wisdom of equality is attained. It is named the wisdom of equality because everything appears impartially and purely, with no differentiation of good or bad, enemies or friends, and so forth.

DISCRIMINATING WISDOM: THE PURIFIER AND PURIFIED

25. *The immediate mentality*
Is called 'the sustainer,' because it sustains the six
    consciousnesses.
It is called 'thought,' because it gives rise to thoughts.
It is defeated by true understanding and the 'illusion-samadhi.'

The seventh consciousness has two aspects: the afflicted and the immediate mind. As previously mentioned, the afflicted mind transforms into the wisdom of equality at the eighth bodhisattva level; however, the immediate mind, along with the sixth, mental consciousness, transforms into discriminating wisdom at enlightenment.

Discriminating wisdom relates to the five sensory consciousnesses and the sixth, mental consciousness. Discrimination of experiences is due to the six consciousnesses, whether the experience arises from one of the five senses or from the mental consciousness. This wisdom knows each thing just as it is and therefore is called "discriminating wisdom," because all experiences of the six consciousnesses are clearly seen.

The immediate mentality is a continuum that causes the arising and cessation of the six sensory consciousnesses, thus sustaining the six consciousnesses, and is therefore known as "the sustainer." Since it also gives rise to thoughts, it is also called "thought." As these thoughts can only be deluded, since the true nature is not realized, they can be eliminated only by true understanding and by the "illusion-samadhi." True understanding realizes the impermanence, suffering, and the emptiness of phenomena. The illusion-samadhi has the knowledge that the mind and its objects are all illusions; therefore, realization of emptiness arises.

DISCRIMINATING WISDOM: THE RESULT OF PURIFICATION

25b. When 'the great patience' is attained.
Due to the transformation of perceptions and perceiver
There is a manifestation of pure realms,
The wisdom of all times,
And total, unimpeded activity.
The thoughts involved in these, transformed
Become 'discriminating wisdom.'

The "great patience," sometimes called the "great equanimity," is the complete and thorough achievement of the perfection of patience, and this is attained at the eighth bodhisattva level, which is called the "unshakable" level. At this stage, the perceiver and what is perceived are transformed so that one can actually enter into the pure realm and can also manifest pure realms to others. At the ninth bodhisattva level, the thoughts of the eighth level transform into unimpeded wisdom of all times, meaning one has the wisdom of the past, present, and future. Finally, at the tenth bodhisattva level, thoughts transform into an unimpeded engagement with all the various kinds of activity required to train beings. The ultimate transformation of all such thoughts into the "discriminating wisdom" occurs at the level of buddhahood, which some systems place at the tenth level and others at the thirteenth level.[37] It is discriminating wisdom knowing all that is to be known, exactly as it is, distinctly and individually.

To summarize, ground consciousness is transformed into the mirror-like wisdom, and the afflicted consciousness, into the wisdom of equality. The sambhogakaya possesses two wisdoms: the wisdom of equality and the discriminating wisdom. The immediate consciousness is transformed into discriminating wisdom.

THE SAMBHOGAKAYA

26. These two wisdoms of equality and discrimination are
Pure meditation, through which there
is no abiding in samsara and nirvana

The possession of peace, love, and compassion;
The manifestation of various bodies;
And teachings to the retinues.
The mandala of the melody of the great dharma is manifest
And a treasury of all samadhis and dharanis.
This is named the sambhogakaya.

After the dharmakaya, which is the realm of complete unimpeded truth that has been described, the sambhogakaya in relation to the wisdom is described. The Sanskrit word, sambhogakaya, literally means "the body of perfect or complete enjoyment" and was trans-lated into Tibetan as *long chö dzok ku. Long chö* means "enjoy-ment" or "pleasures," *dzok pa* means "complete," and *ku* means "body." To understand this word we must ask, "What pleasures does a buddha have?" The sambhogakaya form of the buddha teaches the Dharma to bodhisattvas who have already transcended suffering by attaining the bodhisattva levels. A buddha has the happiness of thinking that he or she has been able to benefit these beings, and is not worried that he or she will slide back into suffer-ing. The activity of a buddha is perfected in the sambhogakaya, in which a buddha is able to present the perfect wisdom, meditation, and activity to bodhisattvas. Therefore, all the pleasures of the Dharma derive from the sambhogakaya.

The essence of the sambhogakaya is the wisdom of equality and the wisdom of discrimination. The wisdom of equality allows the buddhas to see all sentient beings without prejudice, without thinking, "this being is more worthy of enlightenment than that being," so this wisdom gives rise to great compassion. The second, discriminating wisdom allows the buddhas to see everything as it actually is, completely and without any mistakes, so they can engage in flawless buddha activity. We can contrast the sambhoga-kaya with the nirmanakaya, which is the realm we live in presently. Here the buddhas manifest as living beings in five ways. The char-acteristics of the sambhogakaya are, first, a definite retinue that is entirely made up of bodhisattvas who have attained the ten bodhi-sattva levels. In the nirmanakaya, however, a buddha is surrounded by pupils who are more or less diligent, by persons with or without devotion, and by the faithful and the faithless. Second, in the samb-hogakaya there is a definite place, which is the pure realm. A nirmanakaya buddha sometimes manifests in a pure realm and sometimes in an impure realm, whereas a sambhogakaya buddha can only be encountered in a pure realm. Third, there is a certain time that a nirmanakaya buddha and his teachings are presented to the world, whereas a sambhogakaya buddha is present until samsara ends, and his teachings continue without interruption. Fourth, the teachings in the sambhogakaya are exclusively the Mahayana Dharma. A nirmanakaya buddha has pupils at different levels of understanding and introduces them to the Dharma by teaching the definitive teachings to some and the provisional teachings to others, whereas the sambhogakaya buddha teaches only the definitive teachings of the Mahayana. Fifth, a definite teacher is a sambhogakaya buddha. The nirmanakaya buddha possesses the special features of a buddha and has the appearance of being made of flesh and bones, but his body is not composed of physical substance; whereas the sambhogakaya buddha has a completely pure body possessing all the distinctive physical characteristics, and this is his definite body.

These two wisdoms of the sambhogakaya arise from pure meditation, which is beyond samsara and nirvana. The wisdom of equality leads to a great peace and love and compassion for others. The wisdom of discrimination leads to the manifestation of the sambhogakaya deities who reside in the pure realms; for example, Amitabha, who resides in the pure realm of Tushita. In these pure realms, it is said, one hears the continuous teachings of the Dharma, or as the verse says, "the great Dharma melody," which is in the mandala of the pure realm. What is in the mandala of the pure realm? They are all the teachings of the samadhis (meditation) and the *dharanis* (the esoteric Dharma).

THE ALL-ACCOMPLISHING WISDOM

27. The transformation of the five sensory consciousnesses
And the aspect of the mental consciousness are directed
towards them:
The sixteen wisdoms of the 'patience for knowledge'
And the aspects of the four truths,

That have arisen from correct thought,
See and truly realize the meaning.

The all-accomplishing wisdom is associated with accomplishing all the goals of the Dharma, particularly concerning hindrances such as illness and other material obstacles.

The path or map to enlightenment may be described in several ways in terms of the ten bodhisattva levels and in terms of the five paths. The five paths are the path of accumulation, in which we accumulate vast merit and wisdom; the path of junction, in which we are preparing to realize egolessness; the path of insight, in which egolessness is first truly realized and which is the beginning of the ten bodhisattva levels; the path of meditation, in which we develop extremely precise and refined meditation; and the path of no more learning, which is the final path.

The Pramana states that the mental consciousness has two aspects: conceptual and nonconceptual. The five sensory consciousnesses and the nonconceptual aspect of the sixth, mental consciousness, which are impure, are transformed into wisdom through correct examination. Correct examination that has the aspiration for true meditation takes place on the second path, that of juncture. Meditating with that concept of aspiration gives rise to wisdom of the third path, that of insight, and that wisdom sees the nature of the Four Noble Truths: the truth of suffering, the truth of origination, the truth of cessation, and the truth of the path. These truths have two aspects, samsara and nirvana, each having a cause and a result. The result of samsara is suffering, which is described in the first noble truth. The cause of samsara is the disturbing emotions and karma, which is described in the truth of origination. When the disturbing emotions and karma are eliminated, the result of this is a state of peace and liberation that is nirvana, which is described in the third noble truth. The cause of nirvana is the application of the eight-fold method, which is the fourth noble truth.

Each of the Four Noble Truths has four levels of understanding: first, having no true understanding, but the willingness to develop understanding; second, having actual understanding; third, understanding the attainment more thoroughly at the first bodhisattva level; and fourth, attaining complete liberation by having eliminated the mental poisons. These four aspects times the Four Noble Truths are called the "sixteen aspects of the four noble truths" on the third path of insight.

For example, the first noble truth of suffering has first, the obscuration of the nature of suffering, the elimination of which results in the equanimity that understands the nature of suffering; second, having eliminated that aspect, the nature of suffering is seen, resulting in the knowledge of suffering; third, the outcome of attaining the first two aspects is the equanimity of a subsequent understanding of suffering; and fourth, the outcome of attaining all three aspects is the subsequent knowledge of the nature of suffering.

When the first noble truth is seen and we "truly realize the meaning," the elimination of all these obstructions to the truth of suffering is called the "patience for the knowledge of the phenomena of suffering."

> 28. *The five sensory consciousnesses are transformed when:*
> *There is an engagement with all sensory objects,*
> *And the power and possession of the twelve qualities*
> *Of all the bodhisattva levels develop a hundred-fold.*
> *When this is developed to the fullest extent,*
> *It becomes the wisdom of accomplishment.*

Our senses and their corresponding consciousnesses are very limited. For example, when we are inside a room our senses can tell us what is going on in the room, but not what is going on outside the room. Also when we look at an individual, we don't know what that individual's wishes and desires are. However, upon reaching the third path, that of insight, our senses and their corresponding consciousnesses are transformed into all-accomplishing wisdom. When this wisdom is attained we can see the true nature of phenomena, and we can see the nature of other beings—seeing their state of mind, their aspirations, their capabilities, and also seeing what activity is necessary to teach them.

This wisdom is attained on the first bodhisattva level, which is called the "level of complete joy." At this point one attains twelve qualities, and each quality is in a number of a hundred. Some of these twelve qualities are: seeing a hundred buddhas in one instant; receiving the teachings of a hundred buddhas in one instant; manifesting a hundred emanations in one instant; and so on. At the second bodhisattva level, these twelve qualities increase to a thousand-fold; at the third level, they are a hundred thousand-fold; and so on, with their power of benefit increasing until reaching the level of buddhahood and the wisdom of accomplishment. This wisdom is attained at the first bodhisattva level, but it is not complete, because the wisdom of accomplishment is with the nirmanakaya form of a buddha. So this nirmanakaya is not obtained until the complete state of buddhahood. With the wisdom of accomplishment, a buddha knows completely the true nature of phenomena, the nature of his pupils, and the necessary methods required, and so he can effortlessly accomplish the benefit for beings.

THE FOUR TYPES OF NIRMANAKAYA

29. This wisdom accomplishes benefit for all beings
Through an incalculable, inconceivable,
variety of emanations through all realms.
This is the Great Nirmanakaya.

Although the twelve deeds are the principal means by which the supreme nirmanakaya leads beings into the Dharma, the Buddha knew through his clairvoyance what specific individuals needed. Some needed to witness miracles to develop faith and enter the Dharma; therefore the Buddha sent Maudgalyana, one of his principal pupils, to display miracles for them. There were others who were not convinced by miracles but were convinced by logic and reasoning, so he sent Shariputra, who excelled in wisdom, to teach them. Those who were not convinced by either miracles or wisdom, but by excellent restrained conduct, were sent Upali, a monk with excellent conduct, who inspired faith in them. Some would benefit from the Dharma being taught to them, so the Buddha himself would come to lead them into the Dharma. If persons couldn't be brought into the Dharma by the various methods of the supreme nirmanakaya, the Buddha was able to use the created nirmanakaya, which is created for a certain situation, unlike the supreme nirmanakaya that is born, practices meditation, and achieves buddhahood through the path.

The wisdom of accomplishment is the wisdom that accomplishes Buddha activity. The supreme nirmanakaya Buddha accomplished the twelve deeds of the world, which were performed through the wisdom of accomplishment. The reason this wisdom is called the "wisdom of accomplishment of activity" is that whatever needs to be done, can be done. This can only be done after all the ignorance of the five sensory consciousnesses has been transformed, but now whatever needs to be done to benefit oneself or others can be done without any error or mistake. There is the understanding of all things through omniscience.

There are four different kinds of nirmanakaya manifestations: the supreme nirmanakaya, the created nirmanakaya, the born nirmanakaya, and the various nirmanakaya.

The supreme nirmanakaya is, for example, the Buddha Shakyamuni, who appeared in the world and performed the activities that are summarized in the twelve deeds of the Buddha. The Buddha was in the Tushita pure realm before he entered the womb of his mother and took birth in our world to help all beings. He was born in a grove in Lumbini, Nepal, and later accepted his father's kingdom by becoming a prince, marrying a princess, and having a child. He could just as well have descended from Tushita and been born in a flower (as was Padmasambhava), but there is a reason that he did not. If he had been miraculously born, people would have thought, "It is possible for him to achieve enlightenment because he was miraculously born, whereas I am born of an ordinary mother, and therefore cannot achieve enlightenment." If he had not been a prince and had not married, people would have thought, "Being an ascetic is different. I am incapable of becoming ordained and leading a wandering life." However, the Buddha in his nirmanakaya form was born in Lumbini, reached buddhahood at Bodhgaya, and gave Dharma teachings at Varanasi. He taught particular beings with particular actions, until he passed into nirvana.

The second kind of nirmanakaya, the created nirmanakaya, is not born of parents but instead manifests for particular beneficial situations. An example of the created nirmanakaya is a story of Prananda, the king of the *gandharvas*, who are the celestial musicians. He played the *vina*, which is an Indian lute. One day Indra, the king of deities, came to him and said, "The Buddha is in the world now and is giving Dharma teachings. Let's go." Prananda answered, "No, I prefer to practice my vina. You go and enjoy it." Later Indra returned and told Prananda, "The Buddha is halfway through his life. Why don't you listen to the Dharma teachings with me?" Prananda replied, "I will continue practicing my vina. You go." Once more Indra returned and said, "The Buddha is ready to pass away. You had better come now," but Prananda preferred playing his lute.

To break Prananda's attachment and pride, the Buddha manifested as an Indian lute player carrying a lute made completely of lapis lazuli. As he passed by the kingdom of the gandharvas, Prananda heard him playing by the palace gate, and, feeling jealous, said, "Let's compete to see who is the best." They sat down and both played perfectly. Then the Buddha said, "Let's cut one of the strings and then see who plays the best." They played equally well and began cutting more and more strings. When all the strings had been cut, the Buddha's emanation continued playing beautifully, while Prananda could not play. His pride was broken, and he asked, "Where did you learn to play like that?" The Buddha answered, "If you listen to the Dharma teachings of the Buddha, you will be able to play like this too." And so Prananda hurried off to receive the Dharma teachings.

The third kind of nirmanakaya, the born nirmanakaya, is unlike the supreme and created nirmanakaya since one has a body and can take birth as a human or sometimes as an animal. This kind of nirmanakaya does not just teach the Dharma, but benefits beings through their activity or behavior.

Finally, there are various nirmanakaya emanations called *tulkus* in Tibetan, who are not supreme nirmanakayas. For example, the First Karmapa, Düsum Khyenpa, when he was at the end of his life, asked his students to look after his three centers at Tsurphu, Kamaga, and Kampogangara. He told them that he would be reborn and come back and look after these places. Karma Pakshi was born later on, and said that he was the Karmapa. Since he had many miraculous powers, the power of clairvoyance and so on, there was no doubt that he was the second Karmapa. His pupils were very happy, and his return helped them to continue to practice the Dharma. Consequently, when other lamas passed away, their students then went to high lamas and said, "We want our lama to return like Karmapa returned." In response to this, high lamas used their clairvoyant powers to discover where the lama had been reborn, thus helping the students to practice the Dharma. Some tulkus can predict their own birth, as does the Karmapa, and others are recognized by other lamas.

Eventually, there were numerous tulkus in Tibet, some of whom had bad behavior and some who were unintelligent, which made some people wonder whether there was really anything special about tulkus. The tulku may have practiced very diligently and have led a very pure life and so be recognized lifetime after lifetime. However, sometimes a tulku practiced so purely that he or she achieved complete enlightenment and entered into a pure realm. His or her pupils, not knowing this, would go to the Karmapa and ask about the reincarnation, and the Karmapa couldn't say, "He hasn't come back." Instead, the Karmapa would say something like, "Well, maybe this child could be him, and it will be beneficial if you choose him." Believing the child was the tulku, the students would find him, give him training, and his practice would benefit many beings.[38] So before the time of the First Karmapa the use of the word "nirmanakaya" for *tulku* was not used. But from this time on there have been many tulkus, and these make up the fourth kind of nirmanakaya.

THE DHARMADHATU WISDOM AS THE SVABHAVIKAKAYA

30. *Thus mind, mentality, and sensory consciousnesses are transformed*
   Into the three kayas and their activity.
   They are completely present within the mandala of the complication-free dharmadhatu,
   Without samsara, nirvana, or beginning,
   Without being single or multiple.
   This is called 'the essence kaya' (svabhavikakaya).

The origin of all the kayas that we have been discussing is the dharmakaya; more specifically, the aspect of the dharmakaya that is free from all mental fabrications, the svabhavikakaya. In the previous verses, Rangjung Dorje has used three terms for mind rather interchangeably: *namshe* (consciousness), to refer to the eight consciousnesses, and *yi* (mentality) and *sem* (mind). In this verse, however, he uses *sem* (mind) for the eighth consciousness, *yi* (mentality) for the seventh consciousness, and *namshe* for the six consciousnesses.

The eight consciousnesses are transformed into the three kayas: the ground consciousness becomes the dharmakaya, the afflicted consciousness becomes the sambhogakaya, and the other six consciousnesses become the nirmanakaya. Each kaya possesses specific activities: the sambhogakaya assists pure beings to reach the ultimate achievement of buddhahood, the nirmanakaya assists impure beings according to their capacities, and the dharmakaya has the wisdom and love that is the root of all three kayas. Thus, all their activities ultimately derive from the dharmakaya.

Although the dharmakaya is the source of the two wisdoms of the Buddha (the wisdom of the nature of phenomena and the wisdom of their variety) and has love for all beings and has the power of the Buddha's mind, yet it has no true reality. The dharmakaya is empty; its nature is the dharmadhatu, and it is free of mental fabrications. Although the sambhogakaya manifests a form with the thirty-two major and the eighty secondary signs of a supreme being, that manifestation has no true reality and is empty in nature. The nirmanakaya, although it acts to benefit beings, has a nature that is inseparable from the dharmadhatu.

All three of the kayas are beyond conceptual extremes. The dharmakaya is the dharmadhatu and is beyond any conceptual elaboration. Although the sambhogakaya only manifests to bodhisattvas, its essence is also beyond mental elaborations and therefore is also the dharmadhatu. Although the nirmanakaya manifests to impure beings in the form of the Shakyamuni Buddha, its essence is also beyond any mental elaborations and is therefore the dharmadhatu. For this reason all the kayas are undifferentiated in the great mandala of the dharmadhatu, which is called the "essence-kaya" or the "svabhavikakaya." The two aspects concerning realization of the true nature of phenomena are the svabhavikakaya and the dharmakaya, with the svabhavikakaya being the aspect of emptiness and the dharmakaya being the aspect of clarity.

Shantideva (675-725 CE) said that because he taught that all phenomena are empty, some people replied, "If all phenomena are empty, then the Buddha is empty too, so that making offerings to the Buddha will not accumulate any merit. However, although the Buddha indeed has no reality and is just like a dream, an illusory offering made to an illusory Buddha will still result in illusory merit, just as real merit would have arisen from real offerings to a real Buddha."

The three kayas have an empty essence, and this emptiness is called the "dharmadhatu." This dharmadhatu is the fifth wisdom of the five wisdoms, and this wisdom is the absence of any inherent essence or reality. The Sanskrit word *dharmadhatu* was translated into Tibetan as *chö ying*, in which *ying* (Skt. *dhatu*) means "the expanse of space." Space is empty and has the quality of providing room, so without space we could not move. Space allows us to walk, sit, or do any activity. It is combined with *chö*, which is "dharma," so the dharmadhatu is "the space that enables things to happen."

Because the disturbing emotions are pervaded by the dharmadhatu, they don't have any solid reality and thus can be eliminated. If they were truly real, then one couldn't get rid of them. The positive qualities of love and wisdom can be developed because they are pervaded by the dharmadhatu. If they were truly existing, then we wouldn't be able to change them. Thus, we are able to diminish negative qualities and increase positive qualities because phenomena lack any true reality and are pervaded by dharmadhatu; in fact, the eight consciousnesses can be transformed into the five wisdoms because their nature is dharmadhatu.

Many names are given to the dharmadhatu: in the Foundation vehicle it is called the "egolessness or selflessness of the individual," and in the Mahayana it is called "emptiness," but the actual characteristics are explained in the Madhyamaka Shentong school.[39] The Shentong tradition describes both the characteristics and the essence of the dharmadhatu. The word *emptiness* (Skt. *shunyata*) does not mean simply a dead vacuum; rather, in the Shentong teachings the nature of emptiness is taught to be clarity or luminosity. Because of the power of this luminosity, the dharmadhatu is given the name "the essence of the Tathagata" or *tathagatagarbha*, which is often called "Buddha-nature."

All sentient beings possess Buddha-nature, yet they are unable to realize the true nature of phenomena. This is because their dharmadhatu wisdom is covered by two obscurations: cognitive (not realizing the true nature of phenomena) and afflictive (the negative emotions). Just as the sky becomes clear when the clouds have vanished, the wisdom understanding of the true nature of phenomena appears when the afflictions have been removed. Due to the five wisdoms of mirror-like wisdom, the wisdom of equanimity, all-accomplishing wisdom, discriminating wisdom, and dharmadhatu wisdom, the realization concerning the truth of appearances is possible.

One cannot separate the eight consciousnesses and the dharmadhatu. The nature of the dharmadhatu is the eight consciousnesses, and the nature of the eight consciousnesses is the dharmadhatu. This is the same for the two wisdoms; they are all imbued by the dharmadhatu. In Vajrayana meditation this is established by not meditating on the emptiness of external appearances, but meditating on the actual nature of the mind; one is taught to look directly at the mind.[40] For example, if we look at something, we obviously see its appearance in the mind; yet when we try to locate the visual consciousness that is looking, we can't locate it. This is because the nature of the visual consciousness is empty—it is inseparable from dharmadhatu—and we call this "the inseparability of luminosity and emptiness." All the consciousnesses are completely pervaded by dharmadhatu, meaning their nature is also emptiness. The reason we can't find these consciousnesses is that their nature is insubstantial and constantly changing. In the Vajrayana tradition, this is the way we gain the direct recognition of the empty nature of the mind.

We can classify and divide these eight consciousnesses, as we have been doing, using deduction and reasoning; but we cannot actually isolate them when we look for them, because they are the indivisibility of luminosity and emptiness. This emptiness is not a complete voidness, because luminosity is present, thus the process of mind seeing itself is this realization of emptiness. The mental consciousness can allow things to arise in the mind, but the mental consciousness is inseparable from the dharmadhatu and also empty by nature. When these consciousnesses are transformed into the wisdoms, the unity of wisdom and space[41] are established as inseparable.

The four wisdoms that have already been described are therefore pervaded by the dharmadhatu, which is free of mental fabrications. The dharmakaya, sambhogakaya, and nirmanakaya are not new creations; they have always been there. It is this nature, which is known as the fifth dharmadhatu wisdom, that the eight consciousnesses are transformed into. This dharmadhatu wisdom is also a kaya: it is the svabhavikakaya or essence-kaya. The svabhavikakaya, like the dharmadhatu wisdom, is the absence of solid existence that provides space for the other three kayas to occur. That is the nature of the three kayas and why they are called the "essence kayas." Thus Rangjung Dorje said, "multiple or single, this is called 'the essence kaya.'"

OTHER CLASSIFICATIONS OF THE WISDOMS AND THE KAYAS

> 31. *In some other texts, the Victorious One*
> *Teaches this to be the dharmakaya.*
> *The mirror-wisdom is then described as the 'wisdom kaya'*
> *And the other wisdoms as the two 'form kayas'*

This section was written to clear away any doubts students might have. According to the capacities of beings, the Buddha explained the kayas in various ways. Sometimes he spoke of only three kayas, not mentioning the svabhavikakaya, as it was included in the dharmakaya. Sometimes he spoke of the four wisdoms, not mentioning the dharmadhatu wisdom. Sometimes he taught that the dharmadhatu wisdom, the dharmakaya, and the mirror-like wisdom were part of a wisdom-kaya called the *jnanakaya*. Sometimes he taught that the wisdom of equality, discriminating wisdom, and all-accomplishing wisdom were part of the form-kaya called the *rupakaya*, which comprises the sambhogakaya and the nirmanakaya.

In other sutras and texts, the essence-kaya was sometimes called the dharmakaya, because the dharmadhatu is the source of all the qualities of one's own realization and the ability to help other beings. Therefore, the dharmadhatu wisdom was given the name the dharmakaya.

Finally, the mirror-like wisdom was sometimes called the "wisdom kaya." Because it has the aspect of luminosity, the dharmadhatu is sometimes called the dharmakaya. The three wisdoms of equality, discriminating wisdom, and wisdom of all-accomplishment are almost always associated with the two form-kayas (the sambhogakaya and nirmanakaya).

Table 4

The Eighteen Elements or Constituents of Mind
(Skt. dhatu, Tib. khams)

The six objects

1. visual form	rupa	gzugs
2. sounds	shabda	sgra
3. smells	gandha	dri
4. tastes	rasa	ro
5. objects of touch	sparsha	reg bya
6. mental phenomena	dharma	chos

The six sense organs

1. eye sense organ	chakshur-indrya	mig gi dbang po
2. ear sense organ	shrotrendriya	ma ba'i dbang po
3. nose sense organ	ghranendriya	sna'i dbang po
4. tongue sense organ	kayendriya	lus kyi dbang po
5. body sense organ	kayendriya	lus kyi dbang po
6. mind sense organ	mano-indriya	yid kyi dbang po

The eight consciousnesses

1. eye consciousness	chakurvijnana	mig gi rnam par shes pa
2. ear consciousness	shrotravijnana	rna b'i rnam par shes pa
3. nose consciousness	ghranenvijnana	sna'i rnam par shes pa
4. tongue conscious.	jihvavijnana	lce'i rnam par shes pa
5. body consciousness	kayanvijnana	lus kyi rnam par shes pa
6. mental conscious.	manovijnana	yid kyi rnam par shes pa
7. afflicted conscious.	kleshavijnana	nyon mongs rnam par shes pa
8. ground conscious.	alayavijnana	kun gzhi rnam par shes pa

Chapter 6

Summary of the Treatise

This chapter follows the tradition that originated at the great University of Nalanda. When the great panditas of Nalanda wrote commentaries, they described the different ways of relating to the Buddha's teachings. They proposed a method of presenting the subject in a brief summary, which was called "the leap of a tiger." Another method was giving every detail of a teaching word by word, which was called "the crawl of a turtle." There was also a third method of presenting a brief summary of the entire explanation, which was called "the lion returning." This text has been taught according to the crawling turtle method. This summary is the lion returning.

SUMMARY OF THE WISDOMS AND KAYAS

32. Buddhahood is the manifestation of the nature
Of the five wisdoms and four kayas.

When the eight consciousnesses are transformed into the five wisdoms and the four kayas, we become buddhas. Whichever terms are used, there are four kayas: the dharmakaya, sambhogakaya, nirmanakaya, and svabhavikakaya or jnanakaya.

THE TRANSFORMATION OF IMPURE TO PURE

33. That which possesses the stains of the mind,
mentality, and consciousness.
Is described as the ground consciousness.
That which is stainless, is the Buddha-nature.

73

Without the transformation of impure into pure, we are an ordinary being. As an ordinary being we have the mind and mentality and consciousness that are stained with samsara. In this case, there is the ground consciousness, and it is the basis of all samsara. The stains are a part of the consciousnesses, which have already been described as impure, but the mind also has a pure aspect, and this pure, stainless aspect is Buddha-nature.

34. The Buddha has taught that the truth of the path
Is the possession of the power of the Noble Ones,
That is born from the pure conceptualization,
That defeats impure thoughts.

We may ask how we actually transform the eight consciousnesses into the five wisdoms while on the path. The answer is to cultivate pure thoughts, which will automatically defeat impure thoughts. By transforming the eight consciousnesses into the five wisdoms, we come to understand the true nature of phenomena.

In a previous life, when there was a buddha who was also called Shakyamuni Buddha, the Buddha was a poor Brahmin. When he met the Shakyamuni Buddha, he felt great faith in him and wanted to make a connection, so he made an offering of rice soup, even though he didn't have a very nice bowl to put it in. He poured the soup into Shakyamuni's begging bowl; the Buddha drank it and was very pleased. When that happened, the poor Brahmin made a wishing prayer to become just like that Shakyamuni Buddha: to have the exact same body, to teach the same doctrine, and to have the same name. In the future he did become the Shakyamuni Buddha. This demonstrates the necessity of having very pure thoughts and pure motivation.

This transformation happens through the five paths. First, we develop trust and conviction in the Buddha's teachings and enter the path. At this first level of the path of accumulation of wisdom and merit, we begin to understand what the Four Noble Truths are and how we can work with the consciousnesses. On the second path of junction, we receive the teachings, contemplate them, and begin to meditate on them. By the third path of insight, our meditation becomes very pure and we actually see, for the first time, the true nature of phenomena and begin working on "the truth of the path," which are the ten bodhisattva stages. We follow the Noble Ones (Skt. *aryas*) who have realized emptiness. From this the ultimate wisdom arises, and this allows us to thoroughly understand the nature of phenomena.

THE REASON THIS TEXT WAS WRITTEN

35. *The ignorant wander into the ocean of samsara*
    Because they have not realized this ultimate nature.
    Other than with the boat of the Mahayana,
    How could the other shore ever be reached?

Rangjung Dorje concludes by stating the reason that he wrote this text. Normally, we are in a state of delusion and ignorance and darkness. What we need to do is eliminate that state of ignorance and lack of understanding, by transforming the eight consciousnesses into the five wisdoms. If we don't understand the eight consciousnesses and the five wisdoms, then we won't know the path that has to be practiced and the goal that has to be attained; consequently, we will wander in samsara. The Tibetan word for samsara is *khorwa*, which means "to go around" and indicates that in samsara things sometimes are good, sometimes they are bad, sometimes the disturbing emotions become weak, sometimes they become very strong—samsara is just a continuous cycle of happiness and suffering.

Samsara is described by the Buddha as being like an ocean, so we speak of the ocean of samsara. It is said to be like an ocean because an ocean is very vast and very deep and very dangerous. In the time of the Buddha there weren't the boats that we have now, and the only way of traveling on the oceans was in sailboats. Voyages took a very long time, and at the time, it was easy for boats to sink and for passengers to drown. Beings wander on the ocean of samsara because they have not realized the ultimate nature of phenomena or the mind. Crossing it safely requires a great boat. This great vehicle is the Mahayana path. If we can enter and practice the Mahayana, we will be able to cross this ocean of samsara. There is no other means of doing so.

Rangjung Dorje describes his motivation by explaining that he wrote the *Treatise Distinguishing Consciousness from Wisdom* to explain the eight consciousnesses and how they are obscured. But since these consciousnesses can ultimately be transformed into the five wisdoms, he describes them also. Without understanding the eight consciousnesses and their transformation into the five wisdoms, the practitioner will remain in a state of darkness and will not be able to attain freedom from samsara. Both happiness and suffering are experienced in samsara.

Samsara is compared to a bee locked inside a pot. The bee sometimes flies to the top and is stopped by the lid, and since there is nowhere to go, it flies to the bottom again, repeating this pattern again and again. That really is what samsara is like. When sentient beings are in mental darkness, they wander around in samsara's ocean of misery. Rangjung Dorje writes that we need to be free of ignorance. We need to understand the teachings, to contemplate and to meditate on them. By doing this we will become free from ignorance and will be able to cross the ocean of samsara. He wrote this text so that others will understand the nature of all things and be liberated from ignorance. He then concludes with an aspirational prayer:

THE CONCLUDING PRAYER

36. May this meaning be realized by everyone!

We need freedom from delusions of relative reality and the understanding of ultimate reality. If we meditate on the internal mind, we will directly experience its empty nature and its clarity. The realization of the true nature of mind is the direct path of the Vajrayana. Before we engage on this direct path, we must understand the difference between the various consciousnesses and wisdoms. This text does not discuss the Mahayana and Vajrayana meditation practices. It also does not discuss the Mahayana methods of proving the emptiness of all phenomena. The Mahayana sutras clarify the nature of the mind in terms of appearances arising in the mind and the empty nature of these appearances, and this is taught in the text. The Vajrayana view of understanding the mind itself is also presented in the text. Therefore, *Distinguishing Consciousness from Wisdom* is essential for understanding the Mahayana view as well as understanding Vajrayana practice. Rangjung Dorje then concludes with the prayer:

> *May everyone realize the meaning of this text.*
> *May they understand by hearing the teachings*
> *May they develop conviction through contemplation*
>   *and then be able to realize the meaning*
> *of the Lord Buddha's teachings through meditation.*

HOW THIS TREATISE WAS COMPOSED

The Treatise Distinguishing Consciousness and Wisdom was composed in the retreat center Dechen Teng, by Rangjung Dorje on the first day of the tenth lunar month of the year of the pig [the year 1323].

This treatise was composed by Rangjung Dorje, the Third Karmapa. Every Karmapa has his own special kind of activity to benefit his pupils. The First Karmapa excelled in meditation and established the monastic seats of the future Karmapas. The Second Karmapa had very powerful and frightening miraculous powers. The Fourth Karmapa and the Fifth Karmapa had great worldly might and power. The Eighth Karmapa, in contrast, was uninvolved with worldly life and spent a simple life dedicated to meditation.

Rangjung Dorje, the Third Karmapa, was renowned as a great scholar of the sutras and the tantras. He had such great compassion that when he passed away on the fourteenth day of the sixth lunar month in China, he appeared on the next day, the fifteenth, which is the full moon day, within the full moon. This was seen in Tibet as well as China. It gave rise to the tradition of painting Rangjung Dorje's image within a full moon disc. He wrote this text in Dechen Teng, which was a retreat center at Tsurphu, the principal seat of the Karmapa. The other two seats are Kampo Gangra, or Gangchi Rawa, which is in the east of Tibet, near the border with China, and Karma Gön, which was in Kham. Gangchi Rawa had a great sangha, so it was like the body aspect, while Karma Gön had many scholars, so it was like the speech aspect, while Tshurpu had many meditators, so it was like the mind aspect. Around five hundred meditators lived in Dechen Teng at Tshurpu, although since the Chinese Cultural Revolution in 1959 it is in ruins. Rangjung Dorje used to stay there and give teachings to the monks on retreat. It was during one of his residences there that he wrote this text. Therefore it was in a place dedicated to meditation. He gave this teaching on consciousness and wisdom to many great meditators. Therefore this text will be of great benefit to those practicing meditation.

Table 5 (Part I)
The Fifty-One Mental Factors
(Skt. chaitta, Tib. sems byung)

Five Omnipresent Mental Factors (*sarvatraga, kun 'gro*)

1. feeling	vadana	tshor ba
2. discernment	samjna	'du shes
3. intention	chetana	sems pa
4. contact	sparsha	reg pa
5. mental engagements	manaskara	yid la byed pa

Five Determining Mental Factors (*viniyata, yul la byed pa*)

6. aspiration	chhanda	'dun pa
7. belief	adhimokshha	mos pa
8. recollection	smriti	dran pa
9. stabilization	samadhi	ting nge 'dzin
10. superior knowledge	prajna	shes rab

Eleven Virtuous Mental Factors (*kushula, dge ba*)

11. faith	shraddha	dad pa
12. shame	hri	ngo tsha shes pa
13. embarrassment	apatrapya	khrel yod pa
14. detachment	alobha	ma chags pa
15. non-hatred	adveshha	zhe sdang med pa
16. non-bewilderment	amoha	gti mug med pa
17. joyous effort	virya	brtson 'grus
18. suppleness	prasrabdhi	shin tu sbyangs pa
19. conscientiousness	apramada	bag yod pa
20. equanimity	upekshha	btang snyoms
21. non-harmfulness	avihimsa	rnam par mi 'tshe ba

Table 5 (Part II)
The Fifty-One Mental Factors

Six Root Afflictions (*mulaklesha, rtsa nyon*)

22. desire	raga	'dod chags
23. anger	pratigha	khong khro
24. pride	mana	nga rgyal
25. ignorance	avidya	ma rig pa
26. doubt	vichikitsa	the tshom
27. afflicted view	drishti	lta ba nyon bongs can

Twenty Secondary Afflictions (*upaklesha, nye nyon*)

28. wrath	krodha	khro ba
29. resentment	upanaha	'khon 'dzin
30. concealment	mrakshha	'chab pa
31. spite	pradasha	'tshig pa
32. jealousy	irshhya	phrag dog
33. avarice	matsarya	ser sna
34. deceit	maya	sgyu
35. dishonesty	shathya	g yo
36. self-importance	mada	rgyags pa
37. harmfulness	vihimsa	rnam par 'tshe ba
38. non-shame	ahrikya	ngo tsha med pa
39. non-embarrassment	anapatrapya	khrel med pa
40. lethargy	styana	rmugs pa
41. agitation	auddhatya	rgod pa
42. non-faith	astraddhya	ma dad pa
43. laziness	kausidya	le lo
44. non-consciousness	pramada	bag med pa
45. forgetfulness	mushhitasmritita	brjed nges pa
46. distraction	vikshhepa	rnam par g. yeng pa
47. non-introspection	asamprajanya	shes bzhin ma yin pa

Four Changeable Mental Factors (*aniyata, gzhan 'gyur*)

48. contrition	kaukritya	'gyod pa
49. sleep	middha	gnyid
50. examination	vitarka	rtog pa
51. analysis	vichara	dpyod pa

Notes

By Clark Johnson, PhD
(Except where noted)

1. Mahamudra practice involves maintaining complete mindfulness and awareness in one's work, one's social activities, one's eating, sleeping, and so on. It also involves formal sitting meditation in which one looks directly at the nature of the mind.

2. In Tibetan Buddhism there is the practice of certain yogas intended to clear out the subtle channels (Skt. *nadi,* Tib. *tsa*), which are not anatomical but more like meridians in acupuncture in which energies or winds (Skt. *prana,* Tib. *lung*) travel. These energies are closely related to thought, so the practitioner does certain exercises and certain visualizations to enhance meditation. One example of these practices is the Six Yogas of Naropa.

3. In a vast array of studies Western science has shown that the sense organs such as the eye do not simply send a picture of what is on the retina to the brain, but actually send processed information such as size, shape, and contour information to the brain where the picture is reconstructed. This information sent to the brain is not an accurate picture, however, with optical illusions being just one such example of the incorrectness of the picture sent. These sensory faculties located in the brain work simultaneously and not in succession as suggested by the nonBuddhists.

4. Luminosity or luminous clarity (Tib. *salwa)* is a quality of awareness of mind. This will be covered in greater detail in later chapters, but basically it can be shown that the mind is "empty of inherent existence." This means that when we look for where thoughts originate, where they dwell, and where they go when a thought is completed, we cannot find them

anywhere. They are not solid or real; otherwise they would have an origin, a place to dwell, and a place where they would go. However, we know that even though the mind is "empty" it has luminosity or clarity.

5. Egolessness of self (Tib. *dagme*) refers to the fact that when we look for mind i.e. where thoughts arise from, where they dwell, and where they vanish to, we cannot find it. Furthermore, when we look for the consciousness and who is doing the thinking, we again find nothing is there and that the mind is rather an ever-changing stream of thoughts and feelings and not a solid self. We call this realization that we aren't a substantial self or ego the realization of egolessness.

6. Aggregates (Skt. *skandha*) literally means "heaps" or "piles" as in a pile of rocks. In this context they are the five steps of perception. First, a visual image, sound, taste, or other sensory object contacts the sense faculty and this is the first aggregate of form. Second, there is a feeling of accepting or rejecting of this form which is the second aggregate of sensation. The perception is automatically classified as beautiful, pleasant, or desirable or as ugly, threatening, or undesirable, or as simply neutral. The sense perception, of course, is none of these—it is simply a sensory perception. Third, the sensory perception is identified so that one identifies the perception as "a chair" or "my wife" or the like. This aggregate has been translated as "identification" or "discrimination" and this process, of course, involves past experience. After the sensory perception is identified, it is connected with previous conditioning and habitual patterns in the fourth aggregate, which is translated as "formation." So one not only identifies the object, but all one's past history with the object and what it relates to is part of this perception. The last aggregate is consciousness and this occurs when the perception enters the sixth, mental consciousness as a mental object. Although we can divide these aggregates up as distinct units intellectually, they are actually a continuous, indivisible process of perception.

7. Negative emotions are *kleshas*, which in Sanskrit means "pain, distress, and torment." This was translated as "afflictions" which is the closest English word to what causes distress.

However, the Tibetan word for kleshas is *nyon mong* and almost always refers to passion, anger, ignorance, jealousy, and pride, which are actually negative or disturbing emotions, so we prefer the translation "negative or disturbing emotion" since "afflictions" implies some kind of disability. *The Great Tibetan Dictionary* for example defines *nyon mong* as, "mental events that incite one to unvirtuous actions and cause one's being to be very unpeaceful."

8. The numbered verses are a translation of the original root text of Rangjung Dorje.

9. "To listen" to the teachings is the literal translation of the Tibetan *talwa*. Rinpoche has said that in this modern age this actually means "to study" the teachings. Listening, contemplating, and meditating on the teachings are the three wisdoms or *prajnas*.

10. Samsara may be divided into three realms. The lowest level is the desire realm, which is our ordinary existence in which we are dominated by desires. The next level is the form realm, which is being born without having a human body and being non-human because of having attained one of the four concentrations in a previous life. There are the seven god realms. Finally, there is the formless realm where there is pure consciousness.

11. These four schools and their views are given in much greater detail in Thrangu Rinpoche's *An Open Door to Emptiness*.

12. Interdependent origination (Skt. *pratityasamutpada*, Tib. *tendrel*) has also been translated as "interdependence" and as "dependent origination." This is a very important concept since it explains how things happen without the existence of a god or creator. The Buddha suggested simply that everything in the world is related to everything else and when something happens it is due to the relationship between cause and effect. There are actually twelve steps (called the "nidana chains") beginning with birth and going to the twelfth stage of death.

13. The word for "nature" or "inherent nature" (Skt. *svabhava*, Tib. *rang bzhin*), also called "essence," refers to a characteristic that defines an entity and separates it from other entities and is

found in Aristotelian logic in the West. For example, water appears as solid and cold (ice), as transparent and fluid (water), and as hot and vaporous (steam), and these can be said to be the worldly appearances of water. Its essence or true nature is none of these appearances, but in modern terms as two hydrogen atoms combined with one oxygen atom. Another example is that people appear to us as having a whole variety of personalities and behaviors, but only an enlightened being is actually able to see their true nature, which is buddha-nature.

14. Buddhists hold a view quite opposite to common sense or what is held in the West, which is that the world we perceive is not really an accurate reflection of reality, but rather is an illusion or an appearance. What we perceive is relative or conventional truth (Tib. *kunzop*), while an enlightened person can see the world "as it really is" or its ultimate truth (Tib. *dondam*). Ordinary beings see external phenomena as solid and real and experience existence as the continual ups and downs of samsara; while ultimately, external phenomena is not this at all, it is empty.

15. Because one's likes and dislikes are based on past experience and habitual patterns which are stored in the ground consciousness, this needs to be present in perception when there is any recognition of the object. The afflicted consciousness is there because one's mind is still dualistic and this consciousness interprets everything in terms of "I" and "other."

16. The two different natures here are the nature of external phenomena, which are empty even though they appear as substantial objects, and the nature of the mind, which is also empty but has the nature of luminosity or awareness. Because external phenomena have the same nature i.e. are made of the same material, we can build roads, houses, and airplanes with external phenomena. However, mind has a different nature so we cannot build bridges and so on by simply thinking or dreaming them.

17. The complete title is "Explanation of the five sensory consciousnesses accomplishing the sensory objects, without any other creator."

18. The Middle-way or Madhyamaka school of Buddhism in the
    second century CE under the leadership of Nagarjuna devel-
    oped an extremely complex and extensive set of logical argu-
    ments to show that all external phenomena are empty (Skt.
    shunyata). Thrangu Rinpoche tries to give the flavor of these
    arguments using a logical argument known as "the single and
    multiple," showing that everything external that we see and
    think is solid and real is not inherently a "hand" or a "chair" or
    a "mountain," but rather a mental creation of many different
    parts that we think of as a single object.

    A modern example of this argument is that if we hit a brick
    wall with our fist, it will seem solid and we will experience pain.
    Yet a physicist will tell us that the wall is actually 99.99% empty
    space and what little solid matter there is in the wall is atoms
    moving at incredible speeds and one can never even locate the
    position of these atoms. Furthermore, the wall is not "red" but
    simply lets out a radiation that the human mind calls "red." In
    other words, on the relative level it is a solid, red brick wall
    because our mind has taken this impression and made it into a
    red brick wall. However, an advanced practitioner, such as
    Milarepa, could move his body through solid objects because
    his mind had realized that all such objects are, in fact, empty.

19. The word "look" is used here, but clearly this has nothing to do
    with sight. The word is used to contrast it with analyzing or
    examining, which has an analytical, cognitive component that
    isn't present in "looking" at mind. So looking at mind implies
    direct and nonconceptual examination.

20. *Rangrig* is mind looking at itself. To understand this, one has
    to understand the background of Mahamudra practice. In
    mahamudra meditation one begins by first developing tran-
    quility meditation, which trains the mind to focus on an object
    and stay with it without distraction or discursive conceptuali-
    zation. One also develops vipashyana meditation, which in the
    Vajrayana is discovering the true nature of phenomena. These
    two meditations are developed in formal sitting meditation
    while one also engages in trying to achieve complete mindful-
    ness and awareness in post-meditation as well as accumulating
    as much merit as possible.

When these have been achieved to a high degree and one has done the four preliminary ngondro practices to develop devotion, purification, generosity, and devotion to one's guru, one then begins looking directly (nonconceptually) at mind itself to fully realize that mind and self are empty. This then is *rang rig*, and one discovers that one cannot ever find the mind. Of course, what is doing the looking and what is being looked at is the same: mind. Yet with extremely focused meditation it is possible to nonconceptually see the true nature of mind and its emptiness. This is mind seeing itself. For more details see Thrangu Rinpoche's *The Essentials of Mahamudra: Looking Directly at Mind.*

21. The literal name of this heading is "The teaching is that the mind is birthless." Being "birthless" is a characteristic of phenomena, which are empty of inherent existence. "Birth" means it arose at a particular time under a certain cause and result. The mind through all its countless reincarnations has existed as a continuum through ages, just like a mighty river has existed for millennia.

22. This is a jewel that produces anything that is wished for. Thrangu Rinpoche says that in ancient times these did exist, but they do not exist anymore. It is also a metaphor for attaining buddhahood, because all of one's wishes are fulfilled with the attainment of buddhahood.

23. Thrangu Rinpoche gives the example of Milarepa, who meditated diligently and achieved the realization of emptiness. In the *Hundred Thousand Songs of Milarepa* there is the story of two academics who came to Milarepa's cave to discredit him. In reply, he asked them if a rock in the cave was solid and they said, "Of course!" whereupon Milarepa began moving his body through the rock. This was no trick, Milarepa had truly realized emptiness so that this apparently solid world and appearances were no longer solid to him, and he could freely move wherever he wanted.

24. Deva is the Sanskrit word for "god" and refers to someone who has reached a higher birth than a human birth; but since gods are still part of the six realms of samsara, they still have to receive Dharma teachings to reach enlightenment.

25. Latencies (Tib. *pakchak*) or latent imprints enter the eighth consciousness through the seventh consciousness. These imprints are not the experience itself, but are described as more like dormant seeds that are away from soil, water, and sunlight. These imprints are positive, negative, or neutral depending upon whether they came from a positive, negative, or neutral thought or action. These imprints are then activated with experience and thus help create our impression of the solidity of the world. There are actually several kinds of latencies: latencies which are associated with external sensory experiences, latencies which give rise to the dualistic belief of I and other, and positive and negative latencies due to our actions that cause us to continue to revolve around and around in samsara.

It should also be pointed out that different schools of Buddhism treated these latencies differently. The Mind-only school (Chittamatra) founded by Asanga in the fourth century BCE holds that there are eight consciousnesses (as does this treatise) and the latencies are responsible for us remaining in samsara and also experiencing the world as solid and not empty. The Madhyamaka followers of the Sautrantika school hold that there is an objective external reality and that there are only seven consciousnesses and therefore no eighth consciousness. Basically they believe that the seventh consciousness receives these latencies and projects the outside world. Finally, the Madhyamaka followers of the Prasangika school do not hold that there is an external reality and hold that there is no seventh or eighth consciousness. They posit that the self is a conceptual stream that receives these latencies and is involved in the projection of external phenomena. The subject of different schools is, of course, extremely more complicated than this, and there are present day sects in Tibet that adhere to one or another of these views.

26. Western anatomical studies have shown that the sense organs process information and transmit this information to the brain. The retina of the eye, for example, has certain rods that transmit only when the object is round, other rods when it is square, others only when it is moving. So the picture the brain or mental consciousness receives is something like, "round, red,

moving to the left, sharp edges" and not just a picture of what falls on the retina (as happens on a film in a camera).

27. Pönlop Rinpoche has pointed out that anatomical texts describe very closely what Jamgon Kongtrul was describing. For example, the "fine copper hairs" are very similar to the microscopic hairs in the inner ear that are responsible for receiving sound.

28. Here we now have the joining of several strands of Buddhist philosophy: we have the emptiness of external phenomena on the ultimate level as explained by the Middle-way thinkers; we have these external objects as we experience them on the relative level; we have the luminosity of the mind as expounded by the Shentong school; we have the Mind-only view that everything is mind; and we have the Chittamatra view that the eighth consciousness has accumulated these latencies from beginningless time. So over beginningless time, the eighth consciousness has received latencies that these empty external objects are solid and real, and therefore when we perceive an object these latencies tell us that the external phenomenon is solid and real rather than empty. This has been expressed in the *Lankavatara* sutra with:

> *The perception of external phenomena as reality*
> *Is caused by diverse thoughts*
> *Rooted in the psychic residue of past lives.*
> *This is the transitory mind.*
> *It creates all forms.*
> *What appears to be external reality*
> *Is actually nonexistent.*

29. There are two basic ways to develop an understanding of emptiness: analytical meditation (Tib. *je gom*) and placement meditation (Tib. *ne gom*). In analytical meditation one reads (or listens to) a passage giving a logical argument supporting emptiness, and then one goes into a deep shamatha meditation and contemplates this argument. In placement meditation one goes directly into deep shamatha meditation, and then one "looks at mind" directly without any analysis and perceives its emptiness. The analytical method is associated with the sutra approach, and placement meditation is associated with the

Mahamudra or Dzogchen approach to meditation. For more details see Thrangu Rinpoche's *Looking Directly at Mind: The Moonlight of Mahamudra*, Namo Buddha Publications, 2001.

30. Hungry ghosts (Skt. *preta*) are one of the six kinds of beings who inhabit samsara. These beings can only be seen by persons with special clairvoyance or who are highly spiritually evolved. Thrangu Rinpoche teaches that because ordinary beings can't see certain beings, such as hungry ghosts, this does not necessarily mean they do not exist. In fact, the Buddha asked that paintings of the six realms be placed in temples and then bodhisattvas would journey to these realms and come back and describe what they had seen. One can also see these realms as states of mind, with each realm characterized as a particular disturbing emotion. The gods are consumed with pride because they are the most revered beings; the jealous gods are not full gods, so they are consumed with jealousy; humans are greatly concerned with pride and material objects; animals are characterized by ignorance; the hungry ghosts are consumed by desire; and the hell beings are consumed by great hatred and aggression.

More specifically, hungry ghosts were in previous lifetimes very stingy and miserly and motivated by great greed. They were reborn in the ghost realm where they can see food and water all around them, but have a very tiny throat, said to be the size of the eye of a needle, so they cannot fulfill their desire.

31. The difference between mind (Tib. *sem*) and mental factors (Tib. *sem yung*) is that mind is a collection of all that is present in thought, while mental factors are more like long-term dispositions. Mental factors may be positive, such as the ten virtuous factors including faith, shame, and non-hatred; negative, such as the six root afflictions including desire, anger, and pride and the twenty secondary afflictions such as jealousy, avarice, and dishonesty; and neutral, such as the five aggregates, sleep, examination, and analysis. There are fifty-one mental factors in all according to most systems of Buddhist psychology.

–Thrangu Rinpoche

32. Thrangu Rinpoche is employing an argument using Madhyamaka logic, which might not be familiar to Western readers.

For example, if we have a seed and it grows into a tree, the seed is the causal condition and the tree is the effect. When the plant is a tree (the effect), then the seed (its cause) is no longer present.

33. The Tibetan word for "meditation" is *gom* (spelled *sgom*) and the word for "habituation" is *khom* (spelled *goms*). So meditation has the same root as the word for habituation.

34. Maudgalyayana was one of the Buddha's ten main disciples and he tried to lead the third council of the Buddhist teachings. His recitation of the Buddha's words was said to be blocked by demons so Maudgalyayana had to perform miracles to scare off these intruding demons.

35. The complete title of this section is "The mirror-wisdom explained as the dharmakaya, in terms of purifier and purified."

36. The complete title is "The mirror-wisdom: the result of purification—kaya and wisdom."

37. In the Mahayana literature there are only ten bodhisattva levels and in the tantric (Vajrayana) literature there are thirteen levels, which are the ten plus three more subtle stages of manifesting enlightenment. The ten levels are (1) The Joyous One with an emphasis on generosity, (2) The Stainless One with an emphasis on discipline, (3) The Illuminating One with an emphasis on patience, (4) The Flaming One with an emphasis on exertion. (5) The One Difficult to Conquer with an emphasis on samadhi, (6) The Manifest One with an emphasis on wisdom, (7) The Far Going One with an emphasis on skilful activity, (8) The Unshakable One with an emphasis on future, (9) The One of Good Discrimination with an emphasis on efficacy, (10) Cloud of Dharma with an emphasis on attaining enlightenment

38. Thrangu Rinpoche relates: "I have a personal experience of this. I am called Thrangu Tulku. When I first gave this some thought, I was perplexed. I thought, "Well, I know that I'm not Thrangu Tulku, but the Karmapa said that I am! The Karmapa knew my father's name and mother's name, even though I was born far away and he didn't know my family." I thought about

this a lot, and felt that it was all very strange. So one day I asked my *khenpo*, "I know I'm not the Thrangu Tulku, but I've been declared to be him. Why? Perhaps the real one will turn up some day." The khenpo said that there definitely wouldn't be anybody else, but that I knew what my own mind was like, and if I was certain I wasn't a tulku, then I wasn't one!

This left me wondering, "What does all this mean?" until finally I understood. The Karmapa had given me the name of Thrangu Tulku because it would be very beneficial for me. Otherwise, I would have either become a merchant like my father or worked in the fields like my mother. Having been recognized as Thrangu Tulku, I became a monk, received teachings from many lamas, and had the opportunity to practice the Dharma. So he didn't declare me to be Thrangu Tulku because I was the actual tulku, but in order for me to carry on the work of the Thrangu Tulkus, which is what I am now doing.

So we should understand that there is the supreme nirmanakaya, the created nirmanakayas, and the born nirmanakayas, while in the tulku tradition of Tibet, there are superior tulkus, inferior tulkus, and finally counterfeit tulkus like myself!"

–Thrangu Rinpoche

39. Thrangu Rinpoche is one of the foremost scholars of the Shentong tradition, as were Jamgon Kongtrul and Rangjung Dorje before him.

40. This is Mahamudra or dzogchen meditation. This is not as simple as it seems and requires years and years of training.

41. The fifth element is translated as "space" because it supports everything else. This is more like the concept of the fifth element (after earth, water, fire, air) of ether in Aristotelian logic, rather than simply space. In the West the concept of ether or aether was proven not to exist as late as 1881 in a physics experiment.

Table 6

The Ten Bodhisattva Levels

1. The Joyous One (rab tu dga' ba) — Emphasis on generosity (sbyin pa)
2. The Stainless One (dri ma med pa) — Emphasis on discipline (tsultrim)
3. The Illuminating One ('od byed pa) — Emphasis on patience (bzod pa)
4. The Flaming One ('od 'phro ba) — Emphasis on exertion (bzod pa)
5. The One Difficult to Conquer (shin tu sbyang dka' ba) — Emphasis on samadhi (tendzin)
6. The Manifest One (mngon du gyur ba) — Emphasis on wisdom (sherab)
7. The Far Going One (ring du song pa) — Emphasis on skillful activity (thabs la mkhas pa)
8. The Unshakeable One (mi gyo ba) — Emphasis on future projection (smob lam)
9. The One of Good Discrimination (legs pa'i blo gros) — Emphasis on efficacy (stobs)
10. The Cloud of Dharma (chos kyi sprin) — Attaining enlightened wisdom (ye shes)

Glossary

Abhidharma (Tib. *chö ngön pa*) The Buddhist teachings are often divided into the Sutras (teachings of the Buddha), the Vinaya (teachings on conduct), and the Abhidharma (analysis of phenomena, which exist primarily as a commentarial tradition to the Buddhist teachings). There is not, in fact, an Abhidharma section within the Tibetan collection of the Buddhist teachings.

afflicted consciousness (Tib. *nyön yid*) The seventh consciousness. As used here it has two aspects: the immediate consciousness, which monitors the other consciousnesses, making them continuous, and the klesha consciousness, which is the continuous sense of self. See consciousnesses, eight.

afflictions See kleshas.

aggregates, five See skandhas

alaya consciousness (Tib. *künshi namshe*) According to the Chittamatrin school this is the eighth consciousness and is often called the "ground consciousness" or "store-house consciousness" because it stores the latent karmic potentials.

analytical meditation (Tib. *je gom*) In the sutra tradition one begins by listening to the teachings which means studying the Dharma. Then there is contemplation of this Dharma, which is analytical insight and which is done by placing the mind in shamatha and putting the mind one-pointedly on these concepts.

arhat Accomplished Foundation vehicle practitioners who have eliminated the negative emotions or kleshas. They are the fully realized shravakas and pratyekabuddhas.

arhatship The stage of having fully eliminated the klesha obscurations.

arya A person who has achieved direct realization of the true nature of reality. This person has achieved the third (path of insight) of the five paths.

Asanga A fourth century Indian philosopher who founded the Chittamatra or Yogacara school and wrote the five works of Maitreya which are important Mahayana works. Also, brother of Vasubandhu.

Atisha (982-1055 CE) A Buddhist scholar at Vikramashila University in India who came to Tibet at the invitation of the King of Tibet to overcome the damage done by Langdarma. He helped found the Kadam tradition.

atman Sanskrit for a permanent, unchanging "self," which the Hindus believe continues beyond death.

Avalokiteshvara (Tib. *Chenrezig*) Deity of compassion who was known as the patron deity of Tibet; his mantra is OM MANI PADME HUM.

ayatanas These are the six sensory objects such as a sight, a sound, a smell, a taste, and a body sensation; the six sense faculties of the visual sensory faculty, the auditory sensory faculty, etc. and the six sensory consciousnesses such as the visual consciousness, the auditory consciousness, etc. These make up the eighteen constituents of perception.

bodhisattva An individual who is committed to the Mahayana path of practicing compassion and the six paramitas in order to achieve buddhahood and free all beings from samsara. More specifically, those who have a motivation to achieve liberation from samsara for the sake of all sentient beings and achieve the ten bodhisattva levels culminating in buddhahood.

bodhisattva levels (Skt. *bhumi*) The levels or stages a bodhisattva traverses to reach enlightenment. They usually are described as consisting of ten levels in the sutra tradition and thirteen in the tantra tradition.

Bon (Tib.) The religion of Tibet before Buddhism was introduced, which is still being practiced. A practitioner is called a Bonpo.

Brahma A chief god in the form realm.

Brahmin A Hindu of the highest caste who usually performs the priestly functions for Hindu followers.

Buddha-nature (Skt. *tathagatagarba*) The original nature present in all beings which when realized results in enlightenment. It is often called the "essence of buddhahood" or "enlightened essence."

Buddha Shakyamuni The Shakyamuni Buddha, often called the Gautama Buddha, refers to the most recent historical Buddha, who lived between 563 and 483 BCE

Chandrakirti A seventh century Indian Buddhist scholar of the Madhyamaka school who is best known for founding the Prasangika subschool and writing two treatises on emptiness using logical reasoning.

Charvakas A philosophical school in India which rejected the sacred scriptures and vedas, the belief in reincarnation and karma, and therefore advocated hedonism and doing whatever one wants in self-interest.

Chittamatra school Usually translated as the Mind-only school. Founded by Asanga in the fourth century, one of the four major schools in the Mahayana tradition. The main tenet (to greatly simplify) is that all phenomena are mental events.

consciousnesses, sensory (Tib. *bang she*) These are the five sensory consciousnesses of sight, hearing, smell, taste, touch, and body sensation.

consciousnesses, eight (Skt. *vijnana*) The five sensory consciousnesses of sight, hearing, smell, taste, touch, and body sensation; plus the sixth, mental consciousness, the seventh, afflicted consciousness, and the eighth, ground consciousness.

conventional truth There are two truths: relative or conventional truth and absolute or ultimate truth. Conventional truth is the perception of an ordinary (unenlightened) person, who sees the world through false ego-based projections.

clarity See salwa.

definitive meaning The Buddha's teachings that state the direct meaning of Dharma. They are not changed or simplified for the capacity of the listener, in contrast to the provisional meaning.

dependent origination See interdependent origination.

desire realm The abode of the six realms of samsara, so called because its inhabitants are continually tempted by desire. See realms, three.

deva (Tib. *lha*) Sanskrit for god. In this book it refers to a more highly evolved being who is still part of samsara and therefore in need of Dharma teachings to reach enlightenment.

dharma (Tib. *chö*) Dharma has two meanings. We use the lower case dharma to mean phenomena.

Dharma (Tib. *chö*) The second meaning of Dharma, which we capitalize, refers to the teachings of the Buddha.

dharani A short sutra containing mystical formulas of knowledge that are symbolic. They are usually longer than mantras.

dharmadhatu The all-encompassing, unoriginated, beginningless space out of which all phenomena arise. The Sanskrit means "the essence of phenomena" and the Tibetan means "the expanse of phenomena" but usually it refers to the emptiness that is the ground out of which phenomena arise.

dharmakaya One of the three bodies of buddhahood. It is enlightenment itself; that is, wisdom beyond reference point. See kayas, three.

disturbing emotions See kleshas.

doha A spiritual song spontaneously composed expressing a Vajrayana practitioner's realization. It usually has nine syllables per line.

Dusum Khyenpa (1110-1193 CE) The First Karmapa, who was a student of Gampopa and founded the Karma Kagyu lineage. He is also known for founding the tulku system in Tibet.

Dzogchen (Skt. *mahasandhi*) Also known as the "great perfection" or atiyoga. It is the highest of the nine yanas according to the Nyingma tradition. Dzogchen meditation involves looking directly at mind.

eighteen constituents of perception See ayatanas.

emptiness See shunyata.

egolessness (Tib. *dag me*) Also called "selflessness." In two of the Hinayana schools (Vaibhashika and Sautrantika) this referred exclusively to the fact that "a person" is not a real permanent self, but rather is a collection of thoughts and feelings. In two of the Mahayana schools (Chittamatra and Madhyamaka) this was extended to mean there was no inherent existence of external phenomena as well.

five aggregates See skandhas.

five sensory consciousnesses These are the sensory consciousnesses of sight, hearing, smell, taste, touch, and body sensation.

five paths Traditionally, a practitioner goes through five stages or paths to enlightenment. These are: (1) The path of accumulation, which emphasizes purifying one's obscurations and accumulating merit; (2) The path of junction or application, in which the meditator develops profound understanding of the Four Noble Truths and cuts the root to the desire realm; (3) The path of insight or seeing, in which the meditator develops greater insight and enters the first bodhisattva level; (4) The path of meditation, in which the meditator cultivates insight in the second through tenth bodhisattva levels; (5) The path of fulfillment or no more learning, which is the complete attainment of buddhahood.

five wisdoms Upon reaching enlightenment, the eight consciousnesses are transformed into the five wisdoms: the mirror-like wisdom, discriminating wisdom, the wisdom of equality, the all-accomplishing wisdom, and the dharmadhatu wisdom.

form kayas (Skt. *rupakaya*) The sambhogakaya and the nirmanakaya. See kayas, three.

form realm The second of the three realms. In the form realm there are seventeen heavenly realms in which beings have bodies of light. See realms, three.

formless realm The highest of the three realms and the abode of an unenlightened being who has practiced the four absorptions of infinite space, infinite consciousness, nothing-at-all, and neither cognition nor non-cognition. See realms, three.

Foundation Vehicle See Hinayana.

Four Noble Truths The Buddha began his first teaching with the Four Noble Truths at Sarnath, India. These are the truth of suffering, the truth of the cause of suffering, the truth of the cessation of suffering, and the eight-fold path, which make up the foundation of Buddhism.

gandharva A class of deities who are celestial musicians and who live on odors.

Gelug school One of the four main schools of Tibetan Buddhism; founded by Tsong Khapa (1357-1419 CE). His Holiness the Dalai Lama heads this lineage.

geshe (Tib.) A scholar who has attained a doctorate in Buddhist studies. This usually takes twelve to eighteen years to attain.

ground consciousness See alaya consciousness.

Hinayana Literally "lesser vehicle." The term refers to the first teachings of the Buddha, which emphasized the careful examination of mind and its confusion. Also called the Theravadin path or the Foundation vehicle and is the foundation of all Buddhist practice.

hungry ghosts (Skt. *preta*) One of the six types of beings of samsara. Hungry ghosts do not have material bodies, but see all the food and water around them, which they cannot eat or drink. As a result they are always starving and thirsty, and this is the result of excessive greed in their previous lifetimes. See six realms of samsara.

Indra The chief god of the desire realm, said to reside on the top of Mt. Meru.

Insight meditation See Vipashyana meditation.

interdependent origination The principal that nothing exists independently but comes into existence only in dependence on various previous causes and conditions. There are twelve successive phases of this process that begin with ignorance and end with old age and death.

jealous gods (Skt. *asura*, Tib. *lha ma yin*) A type of beings residing in the six realms of samsara who are characterized as being very jealous.

jnana (Tib. *yeshe*) Enlightened wisdom which is beyond dualistic thought.

Kadam (Tib.) One of the major schools in Tibet. It was founded by Atisha (993-1054 CE). A follower is a Kadampa.

Kagyu (Tib.) One of the four major schools of Tibetan Buddhism; founded by Marpa. The other three schools are the Nyingma, the Sakya, and the Gelug schools.

Kamalashila An eighth century scholar in India who was a student of Shantarakshita and is best known for coming to Tibet and debating and defeating the Chinese scholar Hashang Mahayana at Samye monastery and then writing the *Stages of Meditation.*

Karma Kagyu (Tib.) One of the eight schools of the Kagyu lineage of Tibetan Buddhism; headed by His Holiness Karmapa.

Kangyur (Tib.) The 104 volume Tibetan collection of the Buddha's words. The other great Tibetan collection is the Tengyur, which contains the commentaries on the Buddha's teachings.

karma Literally "action." A universal law of cause and effect in which wholesome actions eventually result in improved circumstances, and negative actions eventually result in negative circumstances.

Karma Pakshi (1206-1283 CE) The Second Karmapa, who was known for his miraculous activities.

Karmapa The title of seventeen successive incarnations of Dusum Khyenpa who have headed the Karma Kagyu school of Tibetan Buddhism.

kayas, three A buddha has three bodies: the nirmanakaya, sambhogakaya, and dharmakaya. The dharmakaya or "truth body" is the complete enlightenment or complete wisdom of a buddha, which is unoriginated wisdom beyond form that manifests as the sambhogakaya and the nirmanakaya. The sambhogakaya or "enjoyment body" manifests only to bodhisattvas in the pure realms, and the nirmanakaya or "emanation body" manifests in the world and, in this context, as the Shakyamuni Buddha.

klesha (Skt., Tib. *nyon mong*) Literally "poison." Translated as "afflictions" or "defilements" by some, but in this text as "disturbing emotions" or "negative emotions." The three main poisons are passion or desire, aggression or anger, and ignorance. The five kleshas are the three above plus pride and jealousy.

klesha consciousness (Tib. *nyön yid*) The seventh consciousness, which is responsible for the constant sense of ego or "I." See consciousnesses, eight.

lama (Skt. *guru*) A spiritual teacher.

latent karmic imprints (Tib. *pakchak*) Every action that a person does has an imprint, which is stored in the eighth consciousness. These latencies express themselves later by leaving the eighth consciousness and entering the sixth consciousness upon being activated by causes and conditions.

luminosity See salwa.

Madhyamaka A philosophical school founded by Nagarjuna in the first century CE and based on the Prajnaparamita sutras of emptiness. .

Mahamudra Literally "great seal," meaning that all phenomena are sealed by the primordially perfect true nature. This form of meditation is traced back to Saraha (10th century CE) and was passed down in the Kagyu lineage through Marpa. It is, to greatly simplify, the meditation of examining mind directly.

mahasiddha A practitioner who has a great deal of realization. These were particularly Vajrayana practitioners who lived in India between the eight and twelfth century and practiced tantra. The biography of some of the most famous mahasiddhas is found in *The Eighty-four Mahasiddhas.*

Mahayana Literally "great vehicle." These are the teachings of the second turning of the wheel of Dharma, which emphasize shunyata, compassion, and Buddha-essence.

Maitreya In this text it refers to the bodhisattva Maitreya who lived at the time of the Buddha. Maitreya is presently residing in the Tushita pure realm until he becomes the fifth buddha of this eon.

mandala A diagram used in various Vajrayana practices, which usually has a central deity and four directions. It also denotes a sacred location, such as the mandala of the dharmakaya, and this is how it is used in this text.

Manjushri A meditational deity representing discriminative awareness (Skt. *prajna*) and known for knowledge and learning.

Usually depicted as holding a sword in the right hand and scripture in the left.

Maudgalyayana One of the Buddha's ten main disciples.

mental consciousness The sixth consciousness, responsible for analyzing the sensory perceptions of the five sensory consciousnesses. See consciousnesses, eight.

mental factors (Tib. *sem yung*) Mental factors are contrasted to mind in that they are more long-term propensities of mind. These include eleven virtuous factors such as faith, detachment, and equanimity, the six root defilements such as desire, anger, and pride, and the twenty secondary defilements such as resentment, dishonesty, and harmfulness.

Middle-way school See Madhyamaka.

Milarepa (1040-1123 CE) Milarepa was a student of Marpa who attained enlightenment in one lifetime. His student Gampopa founded the (Dagpo) Kagyu lineage.

Mind-only school See Chittamatra school.

mind poisons (Tib. *duk*) See kleshas.

nadi (Skt., Tib. *tsa*) Subtle non-anatomical channels that psychic energies or winds (Skt. *prana*, Tib. *lung*) travel through.

Nagarjuna An Indian scholar in the first century who founded the Madhyamaka philosophical school, which emphasized emptiness.

Nalanda A great monastic Buddhist university from the fifth to the tenth century, located near modern Rajagriha, which was the seat of the Mahayana teachings. Many great Buddhist scholars taught there.

Naropa (956-1040 CE) An Indian pandita who is best known for transmitting many Vajrayana teachings to Marpa, who later took these teachings back to Tibet to help found the Kagyu lineage.

nirmanakaya (Tib. *tulku*) See kayas, three.

nirvana Literally "extinguished." Beings who live in samsara can, with spiritual practice, attain a state of enlightenment in which all false ideas and conflicting emotions have been extinguished. This is called nirvana.

ngöndro (Tib. pronounced "nundro") Tibetan for "preliminary practice." One usually begins the vajrayana path by doing the four preliminary practices, which involve about 100,000 refuge prayers and prostrations, 100,000 vajrasattva mantras, 100,000 mandala offerings, and 100,000 guru yoga practices.

Noble Truths, Four See Four Noble Truths.

Nyingma (Tib.) The oldest school of Buddhism in Tibet, based on the teachings of Padmasambhava and others in the eighth and ninth centuries of this era.

obscurations, two The obscuration of conflicting emotions and the obscuration of knowledge.

Padmasambhava (Tib. *Guru Rinpoche*) He was invited to Tibet in the eighth century CE and is known for pacifying the non-Buddhist forces and founding the Nyingma lineage.

pandita A great scholar.

paramita, six Sanskrit for "perfections," and the Tibetan literally means "gone to the other side." These are the six practices of the Mahayana path: Transcendent generosity, transcendent discipline, transcendent patience, transcendent exertion, transcendent meditation (*dhyana*), and transcendent knowledge (*prajna*). The ten paramitas are these plus skillful means, aspirational prayer, power, and pure wisdom (Tib. *yeshe*).

path The path refers to the process of attaining enlightenment. Path may also refer to part of the threefold logic of ground, path, and fruition.

paths, five See five paths.

placement meditation This is the meditation of directly observing the mind without engaging in any analytical or intellectual activity. This meditation is associated with mahamudra meditation and it contrasts to analytical meditation.

poisons, three The three major defilements: desire or attachment, anger or aggression, and ignorance or bewilderment.

prajna (Tib. *sherab*) In Sanskrit prajna means "perfect knowledge," but here the word means more nearly "intelligence" because it can refer to simply mastering a subject intellectually as well as full realization of the ultimate nature of reality. In this treatise it usually means the wisdom of seeing things from a non-dualistic view.

Prajnaparamita The Buddhist literature outlining the Mahayana path and emptiness, written mostly around the second century.

Pramana Sometimes called "valid cognition." It is the study of the theory of knowledge.

pratyekabuddha Literally "solitary realizer." A realized Hinayana practitioner who has achieved the wisdom of the nature and the wisdom of the variety of phenomena.

prana (Tib. *bindu*) Life supporting energy.

provisional meaning The teachings of the Buddha which have been simplified or modified to the capabilities of the audience. This contrasts with the definitive meaning.

pure realm Realms created by buddhas, which are totally free from suffering and where Dharma can be received directly. These realms are presided over by various buddhas such as Amitabha, Avalokiteshvara, and Maitreya, who preside over Tushita.

Rangjung Dorje (1284-1339 CE) The Third Karmapa, known for his great scholarship. He wrote the *Aspirational Prayer for Mahamudra*, the *Profound Inner Meaning*, a *Treatise on Buddha-essence*, and this text.

realms, three The lowest realm is the desire realm, where beings are dominated by desire. It comprises humans, animals, and hungry ghosts. The next realm is the form realm, where beings don't have a body and are free of gross pain and pleasure. The highest realm is the formless realm, which can only be reached as the result of a previous meditational accomplishment.

Rinpoche (Tib.) Literally "very precious." A term of respect for a Tibetan lama who is a recognized incarnation.

rishi A holy Hindu sage or saint.

rupakaya The form body, which encompasses the sambhogakaya and the nirmanakaya.

Sakya One of the four major schools of Tibetan Buddhism, it was established by Drogmi Lotsawa in the eleventh century.

salwa Tibetan for "luminosity" or "clarity." In the Vajrayana everything is void, but this voidness is not completely empty because it has luminosity. Luminosity or clarity allows all phenomena to appear and is a characteristic of emptiness (Skt. *shunyata*).

samadhi Also called "meditative absorption" or "one-pointed meditation." The highest form of meditation.

sambhogakaya See kayas, three.

samsara (Tib. *khorwa*) Conditioned existence, which is characterized by suffering because one is still afflicted by passion, aggression, and ignorance. It is contrasted to nirvana.

sangha These are the companions on the path. They may be the persons on the path or the noble sangha, which are the realized bodhisattvas.

Saraha A ninth century siddha who was one of the eighty-four mahasiddhas of India. He is known for his spiritual songs about Mahamudra.

Sautrantika school One of the four major schools of Indian Buddhism. This is a Hinayana school.

self-knowledge (Tib. *rang rig*) This is a high meditation in which one looks directly at mind itself with no conceptualization, to determine the characteristics of reality.

selflessness See egolessness.

Shakyamuni Buddha The Shakyamuni Buddha, often called the Gautama Buddha, refers to the latest Buddha, who lived between 563 and 483 BCE

Shamatha (Tib. *shinay*) A basic meditation practice that tames the mind and allows it to stay or rest on a point without being distracted. It is also called "tranquility" or "basic sitting" meditation. The other basic meditation is vipashyana or insight meditation.

Shantarakshita (eighth century CE) An abbot of Nalanda University who was invited by King Trisong Detsen to come to Tibet. He established Samye Monastery and thus helped introduce Buddhism in Tibet.

Shantideva (675-725 CE) A great bodhisattva who lived in the seventh and eighth century in India, known for his two works on the conduct of a bodhisattva.

Shariputra One of the Buddha's ten main disciples. He is known for his intelligence and when the sutras say, "Thus have I heard..." it is Shariputra who recited this sutra.

shastra (Tib. *tenchö*) The Buddhist teachings are divided into words of the Buddha (the sutras) and the commentaries by others on his works (shastras).

shravaka Literally "those who hear." A type of realized Hinayana practitioner (*arhat*) who has achieved the realization of the nonexistence of a personal self.

Shentong school (Tib.) The Madhyamaka or Middle-way school is divided into two major schools: the Rangtong, which maintains emptiness is devoid of inherent existence, and the Shentong, which maintains emptiness is indivisible from luminosity.

shunyata Usually translated as voidness or emptiness. The Buddha taught in the second turning of the wheel of Dharma that all external phenomena and all internal phenomena such as the concept of self or "I" have no real inherent existence and therefore are "empty."

six realms of samsara These are the possible types of rebirths for beings in samsara and are: the god realm, in which gods have great pride, the asura realm, in which the jealous gods try to maintain what they have, the human realm, which has the possibility of achieving enlightenment, the animal realm, characterized by stupidity, the hungry ghost realm, characterized by great craving, and the hell realm, characterized by aggression.

sixteen aspects of the four noble truths These are suffering, impermanence, emptiness, selflessness, the origin of suffering, production, causal basis, condition, cessation, tranquility, excellence, disillusionment with samsara, path, reason, attainment, and the act of becoming disillusioned with samsara.

skandhas Literally "heaps." This is a five-fold category of phenomena—the five basic transformations that perceptions undergo when an object is perceived—form, feeling perception, formation, and consciousness. First is form, which includes all sounds, smells, etc.—everything that is direct perception without concept. The second and third are sensations (pleasant and unpleasant, etc.) and perception. The fourth is formation, which actually includes the second and third aggregates. The fifth is ordinary consciousness, such as the sensory and mental consciousnesses.

spiritual song See doha.

subtle channel See nadi.

sutra Foundation and Mahayana texts that are the Buddha's words. They are often contrasted with the tantras, which are the Buddha's Vajrayana teachings, and the shastras, which are commentaries by others on the words of the Buddha.

sutrayana The sutra approach to achieving enlightenment, which includes the Hinayana and the Mahayana.

svabhavikakaya The essence body, which refers to the dharmakaya.

tantra One can divide Tibetan Buddhism into the sutra tradition and the tantra tradition. The sutra tradition primarily involves the academic study of the Mahayana sutras and the tantric path primarily involves practicing the Vajrayana practices. The tantras are primarily the texts of the Vajrayana practices.

tathagata Literally "those who have gone to thusness." A title for the Buddha.

tathagatagarba Also called Buddha-essence or Buddha-nature. The seed or essence of tathata (suchness).

Tengyur (Tib.) The great Tibetan collection of 108 works of the commentaries (shastra) of the Buddhist works. See Kangyur.

terma (Tib.) Literally "hidden treasure." Works that were hidden by great bodhisattvas and later rediscovered. They might be actual physical texts or they may come "from the sky" as transmissions from the sambhogakaya. A discoverer of these texts is called a terton.

Theravada school See Hinayana.

Theravadin A follower of the Theravada school.

three realms See realms, three.

Tilopa (928-1009 CE) One of the eighty-four mahasiddhas, who became the guru of Naropa. His teachings became the basis of the Kagyu lineage in Tibet.

Tranquility meditation See shamatha.

Tripitaka Literally the "three baskets." There are the sutras (the narrative teachings of the Buddha), the Vinaya (a code for monks and nuns) and the Abhidharma (philosophical background of the Dharma).

tulku (Tib., Skt. *nirmanakaya*) A manifestation of a buddha that is perceived by an ordinary person. The term has commonly been used for a discovered rebirth of any teacher.

Tushita This is one of the heavenly abodes of the Buddha. Tushita is in the sambhogakaya and therefore does not have a specific location.

twelve deeds of the Buddha The life of the Buddha is often summarized in twelve major deeds.

two truths There is the conventional or relative truth, which is the world as we normally experience it with solid objects. The other truth is ultimate or absolute truth, which is mind free of all obscurations and defilements, and inherently empty.

ultimate truth The ultimate truth, which can only be perceived by an enlightened individual, is that all phenomena both internal (thoughts and feelings) and external (the outside physical world) do not have any inherent existence.

Upanishads Pre-Buddhist Hindu religious texts dating from the seventh century BCE.

Vaibhashika One of four main Hinayana schools, with the other three being the Sautrantika, Chittamatra, and Madhyamaka schools. This school held that matter is real or independently existing and is composed of particles, and that time is real and composed of moments, which then compose consciousness.

vajra (Tib. *dorje*) Usually translated "diamond like." A hand held implement used during certain Vajrayana practices and ceremonies; or a quality that is so pure and so enduring that it is like a diamond.

Vajrayana There are three major traditions of Buddhism (Hinayana, Mahayana, Vajrayana). The Vajrayana, which is based on the tantras, emphasizes the clarity aspect of phenomena and is mainly practiced in Tibet.

Vasubandhu A great fourth century Indian scholar who was Asanga's brother and wrote the Hinayana work the *Abidharmakosha* explaining the Abhidharma.

Vinaya The Buddha's teaching concerning proper conduct. There are seven main precepts that may be observed by laypersons, 125 that are observed by monks, and 320 that are observed by nuns.

Vipashyana meditation Sanskrit for "insight meditation," in which one develops insight into the nature of mind. In the Theravada tradition this involves observing every thought in daily life. In the Vajrayana it involves more a close examination of the emptiness of phenomena. The other main meditation is tranquility or shamatha meditation.

wisdom of the nature of phenomena (Tib. *ji ta ba*) This is transcendent knowledge (jnana) of the true nature of reality, not as it appears in samsara.

wisdom of the variety of phenomena (Tib. *ji nye pa*) This is the transcendent knowledge (jnana) of the variety of phenomena.

wish-fulfilling jewel A jewel said to exist in the naga or deva realms which gave the owner whatever he or she wanted. Now used mostly metaphorically.

yana Literally "vehicle." Refers here to a level of teaching. There are three main yanas. See Hinayana, Mahayana, and Vajrayana.

yoga Literally "union." In this text it refers to special movement and breathing exercises that are done to enhance meditation by clearing the subtle channels.

Glossary of Tibetan Terms

Note: There is no standard way to pronounce Tibetan.

Pronounced	Spelled	English
bardo thodrol	bard do'i thos grol	"Book of the Dead"
chö	chos	Dharma
dag me	dbag med	selflessness
dorje	rdo rje	vajra
drubgya	sgrub rgyud	practice lineage
dzog chen	rdzogs chen	great perfection
ji nye pa	ji snyed pa	wisdom of variety
ji ta ba	ji lta ba	wisdom of phenomena
kagyu	bka' brgyud	Kagyu sect
khenpo	mkhan po	abbot
khorwa	'khor ba	samsara
kunshi namshe	kun gzhi' rnam shes	alaya conscious
lama	bla ma	guru
lha	lha	god
lhag tong	lhag mthog	vipashyana
nam shé	rnam shes	consciousness
ngedon	nges don	definitive meaning
nyön mon	gnyon mongs	klesha
nyön yi	nyon yid	klesha conscious.
pak chak	bag chags	latencies
salwa	gsal ba	luminosity
sem	sems	mind
shinay	zhi gnas	shamatha
tong pa nyi	stong pa nyid	emptiness
yeshe	ye shes	wisdom
yi	yid	mind
yi kyi namshe	yid kyi rnam shes	mental consciousness

Books by Thrangu Rinpoche

Creation and Completion

Crystal Clear: Practical Advice for Mahamudra Meditators

Distinguishing Dharma and Dharmata

Essential Practice: Lectures on Kamalashila's Stages of Meditation

Essentials of Mahamudra: Looking Directly at Mind

Everyday Consciousness and Primordial Awareness

Four Foundations of Buddhist Practice

The Heart of the Dharma: Mind Training for Beginners

The Jewel Ornament of Liberation

Journey of the Mind

King of Samadhi: Commentaries on the Samadhi Raja Sutra

Medicine Buddha Teachings

The Middle-Way Meditation Instructions of Mipham Rinpoche

The Ninth Karmapa's Ocean of Definitive Meaning

On Buddha Essence: A Commentary on Rangjung Dorje's Treatise

An Ocean of the Ultimate Meaning: Teachings on Mahamudra

The Open Door to Emptiness

The Ornament of Clear Realization

Pointing Out the Dharmakaya

The Practice of Tranquillity and Insight

Rechungpa: A Biography of Milarepa's Disciple

Shentong and Rangtong: Two Views of Emptiness

Showing the Path to Liberation

A Song for the King: Saraha on Mahamudra Meditation

The Three Vehicles of Buddhist Practice

Transcending Ego: Distinguishing Consciousness from Wisdom

The Uttaratantra: A Treatise on Buddha-Essence

Vivid Awareness: The Mind Instructions of Khenpo Gangshar

Annotated Bibliography

An Adornment for Rangjung Dorje's Thoughts by Jamgon Kongtrul. This is a commentary on Rangjung Dorje's *Distinguishing Consciousness from Wisdom* and has not been translated into English.

The Buddha Within by S. K. Hookham (Albany: State University of New York Press, 1991). Hookham gives an extensive commentary on the Shentong point of view of Buddha-nature. She also translates part of Jamgon Kongtrul's commentary on the Uttara Tantra.

Essentials of Mahamudra: Looking Directly at the Mind by Thrangu Rinpoche (Boston: Wisdom Publications, 2004).

A Handbook of Tibetan Culture by Graham Coleman (London: Rider, 1993). This book lists a great number of Buddhist centers around the world, gives biographies of many Tibetan lamas, and has an excellent glossary.

The Holographic Universe by Michael Talbot (Harper and Collins, 1991). This book summarizes the evidence that everything in the universe is related to everything else in the same manner that a small portion of a hologram contains the information on the entire object, but in less detail. He suggests that human awareness is similar to a laser which is the light source for the physical hologram.

The Hundred Thousand Songs of Milarepa. (Tib. *mila khabum*) by Tsang Myon Heruka translated into English by Chang, Garma C. C. (Secaucus, New Jersey: University Books, 1962). Milarepa was one of the greatest yogis to have ever lived. He taught by singing spontaneous spiritual songs and this is a collection of these realizations.

The King of Samadhi by the Buddha. (Skt. *Samadhi-raja-sutra*). This is one of the few teachings of the Buddha that discusses mahamudra meditation. The first four chapters of this sutra have been translated by John Rockwell at Naropa Institute and the eleventh chapter was translated by Mark Tatz in his PhD thesis at the University of Washington. Thrangu Rinpoche has given an extensive commentary on this sutra in *King of Samadhi* (Boudhanath, Nepal: Rangjung Yeshe Publications, 1994).

Masters of Mahamudra: Songs and Histories of the Eighty-Four Buddhist Siddhas by Keith Dowman (Albany, NY: State University of New York Press, 1985). Keith Dowman translates and gives an extensive commentary on the work by Abhayadatta.

Perfection of Wisdom Literature by the Buddha. There is a Prajnaparamita text of 100,000 verses, a text of 25,000 verses, a text of 8,000 verses, the Heart sutra of only a few verses, right on down to a single seed syllable, AH. The *Perfection of Wisdom* in 8,000 verses (Skt. *ashtasahasrika-prajna-paramita-sutra*) has been translated in *The Large Sutra on Perfect Wisdom* by Edward Conze (Berkeley: University of California Press, 1975).

The Practice of Tranquillity and Insight by Thrangu Rinpoche (Ithaca, NY: Snow Lion Publications, 1993). This book gives an extensive treatment of meditation based on a chapter in Jamgon Kongtrul's *Treasury of Knowledge*.

The Profound Inner Meaning by Rangjung Yeshe. (Tib. *sabmo nang don*). This text is an explanation of the subtle channels and energies that move within them and how this relates to meditation.

The Self-Aware Universe: How Consciousness Creates the Material World by Amit Goswami (New York: Putnam, 1993). This book summarizes a number of modern experiments in physics that show that human consciousness or awareness is necessary for determining the characteristics of matter at least at an atomic level.

The Stages of Meditation by Kamalashila (Skt. *bhavanakrama*, Tib. *sgom pa'i rim pa*). This text in three volumes was written by Kamalashila (8th century CE) and laid the foundation for teaching the gradual path in Tibetan Buddhism. The first book was translated by Giuseppe Tucci in *Minor Buddhist Texts*, Part II (Serie Orientale Roma, IX.2. Rome: Is. M. E. O., 1958).

The Tantra of the Vajra View. This text has not been translated into English.

The Tibetan Book of the Dead (Tib. *bard do'i thos grol*, pronounced *bardo thodrol*) This text was composed by Padmasambhava and written down by his consort Yeshe Tsogyal and hidden as a hidden treasure (Tib. *terma*). It was uncovered by Karma Lingpa. It is a text for achieving liberation while in the bardo state between death and a new rebirth. The first translation was by Evans-Wentz, the second was by Francesca Fremantle and Chogyam Trungpa Rinpoche and a recent version has been published by Robert Thurman. See *The Tibetan Book of the Dead: The Great Liberation Through Hearing in The Bardo*, Fremantle and Trungpa (Boston: Shambhala, 1987).

The Treasury of the Abhidharma by Vasubandhu (Skt. *abhidharma-kosha*, Tib. *chos mngon pa'i mdzod*) Vasubandhu's great summary and commentary on the Abhidharma. This text was greatly respected in Tibet and is the main text used to study the Abhidharma. A detailed study of this work has been published by Sukomal Chaudhuri in his *Analytical Study of the Abhidharmakosa* (Calcutta: Firma KLM, 1983).

The Treatise Distinguishing Consciousness from Wisdom by Rangjung Dorje (Tib. *rnam shes ye shes 'byed pa*, pronounced *namshe yeshe gepa*).

The Treatise Elucidating Buddha-Nature by Rangjung Dorje. This is a short spiritual song written by Rangjung Dorje that summarizes the teachings on buddha-nature. See *On Buddha Essence: A Commentary on Rangjung Dorje's Treatise*, containing a translation of this spiritual song and a commentary by Thrangu Rinpoche (Boston: Shambhala, 2006).

The Upanishads. These are about one hundred Hindu religious texts dating from the seventh century BCE. One of the earliest and most important Upanishads was the Brihadavanyaka written in prose and concerned with the nature of the universe. These have been translated several times into English. See Alistair Shearer and Peter Russell, *The Upanishads* (New York: Harper and Row, 1978).

The Uttara Tantra by Maitreya (Skt. *ratnagotravibhaga,* Tib. *rgyud bla ma,* pronounced *gyu lama).* This text was written in about the fourth century by Asanga, who received a transmission from the bodhisattva Maitreya. For a translation of this text and a commentary by Thrangu Rinpoche see *The Uttaratantra: A Treatise on Buddha-Essence* (Auckland: Namo Buddha & Zhyisil Chokyi Ghatsal, 2003).

A Brief Biography of Thrangu Rinpoche

The lineage of the Thrangu incarnations began in the 15th century when the seventh Karmapa, Chodrak Gyatso, visited the region of Thrangu in Tibet. At this time His Holiness Karmapa established Thrangu Monastery and enthroned Sherap Gyaltsen as the first Thrangu Rinpoche, recognizing him as the re-established emanation of Shuwu Palgyi Senge, one of the twenty-five great siddha disciples of Guru Padmasambhava.

Khenchen Thrangu Rinpoche is the ninth incarnation of this lineage and was born in Kham, Tibet in 1933. When he was four, H.H. the 16th Gyalwa Karmapa and the Palpung Situ Rinpoche recognized him as the incarnation of the Thrangu Tulku by prophesying the names of his parents and the place of his birth.

Entering Thrangu monastery, from the ages of seven to sixteen he studied reading, writing, grammar, poetry, and astrology, memorized ritual texts, and completed two preliminary retreats. At sixteen, under the direction of Khenpo Lodro Rabsel, he began the study of the three vehicles of Buddhism while staying in retreat.

At twenty-three Rinpoche received full ordination from the Karmapa. When he was twenty-seven he left Tibet for India at the time of the Communist military takeover. He was called to Rumtek, Sikkim where the Karmapa had his seat in exile. At thirty-five Rinpoche took the geshe examination before 1500 monks at Buxador monastic refugee camp in Bengal and was awarded the degree of Geshe Lharampa. On his return to Rumtek he was named Abbot of Rumtek monastery and the Nalanda Institute for Higher Buddhist studies at Rumtek. He has been the personal teacher of the four principal Karma Kagyu tulkus: Shamar Rinpoche, Situ Rinpoche, Jamgon Kongtrul Rinpoche, and Gyaltsab Rinpoche.

Thrangu Rinpoche has centers in Asia, Europe, and North America and has traveled extensively throughout the world to teach. In 1984 he spent several months in Tibet where he ordained over 100 monks and nuns and visited several monasteries. In Nepal, Rinpoche founded the Thrangu Tashi Choling monastery and the Shree Mangal Dvip boarding school, for the general education of lay children and young monks, in Boudha; Thrangu Tara Abbey, a monastic college for nuns, in Swayambhunath; the Thrangu Tashi Yangtse monastic college, retreat center, and medical clinic at Namo Buddha, east of the Kathmandu Valley; and the Thrangu Shekhar retreat center in Bhaktapur, just below a cave where Tibetan yogi Milarepa practiced. In India, he has completed the Vajra Vidya monastic college near Deer Park in Sarnath, where Shakyamuni Buddha gave his first teaching on the Four Noble Truths. In North America, Rinpoche is the abbot of Gampo Abbey, Nova Scotia, Canada and has established the Thrangu monastery in Vancouver, B.C., Canada and the Vajra Vidya retreat center in Crestone, Colorado, USA.

Thrangu Rinpoche is one of the most highly regarded masters of mahamudra meditation. He has touched the lives of students from all parts of the world through his compassionate presence, his immense knowledge, and his way of making even complex teachings accessible.

Because of his vast knowledge of the Dharma, Rinpoche has been appointed by His Holiness the Dalai Lama to be the personal tutor for the 17th Gyalwa Karmapa, Orgyen Thinley.

FOR MORE INFORMATION SEE **WWW.RINPOCHE.COM**

Index

117